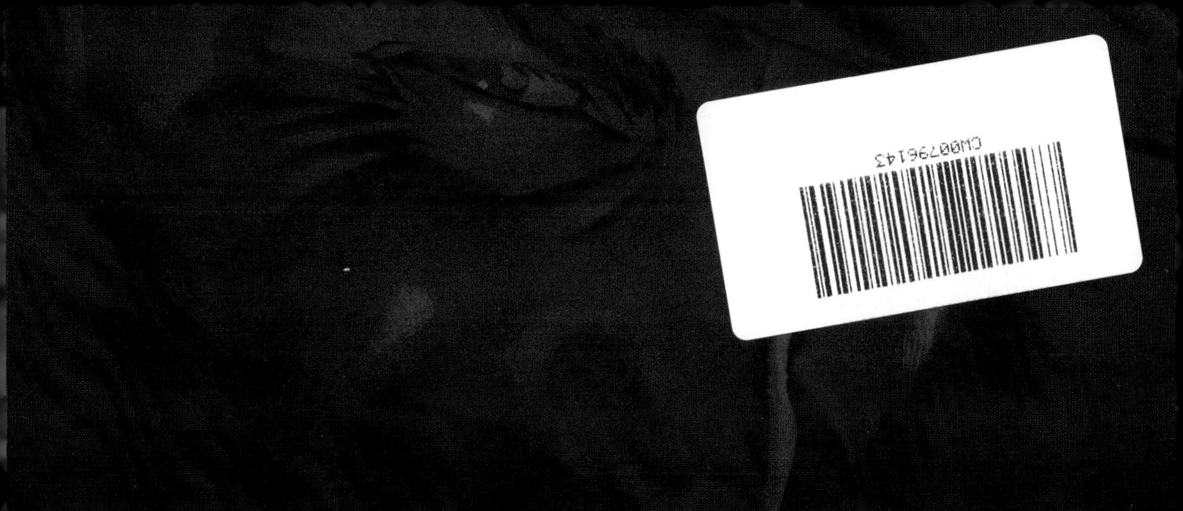

THE Shadow®
DEATH FACTORY

WRITTEN BY **PHIL HESTER**

ART BY **IVAN RODRIGUEZ**

COLORS BY **IMPACTO STUDIOS**

LETTERS BY **ROB STEEN**

COVER BY **PHIL HESTER**

SPECIAL THANKS TO **JERRY BIRENZ, ANTHONY TOLLIN AND MICHAEL USLAN**

THE SHADOW CREATED BY **WALTER B. GIBSON**

DYNAMITE®

Nick Barrucci, CEO / Publisher
Juan Collado, President / COO
Rich Young, Director Business Development
Keith Davidsen, Marketing Manager

Joe Rybandt, Senior Editor
Hannah Elder, Associate Editor
Molly Mahan, Associate Editor

Jason Ullmeyer, Design Director
Katie Hidalgo, Graphic Designer
Chris Caniano, Digital Associate
Rachel Kilbury, Digital Assistant

Online at **www.DYNAMITE.com**
On Twitter **@dynamitecomics**
On Facebook **/Dynamitecomics**
On YouTube **/Dynamitecomics**
On Tumblr **dynamitecomics.tumblr.com**

888-COMIC-BOOK
comicshoplocator.com

THE SHADOW® SPECIAL 2014: DEATH FACTORY. First printing. Published by Dynamite Entertainment, 113 Gaither Dr., STE 205, Mt. Laurel, NJ 08054.

For information regarding press, media rights, foreign rights, licensing, promotions, and advertising e-mail: marketing@dynamite.com

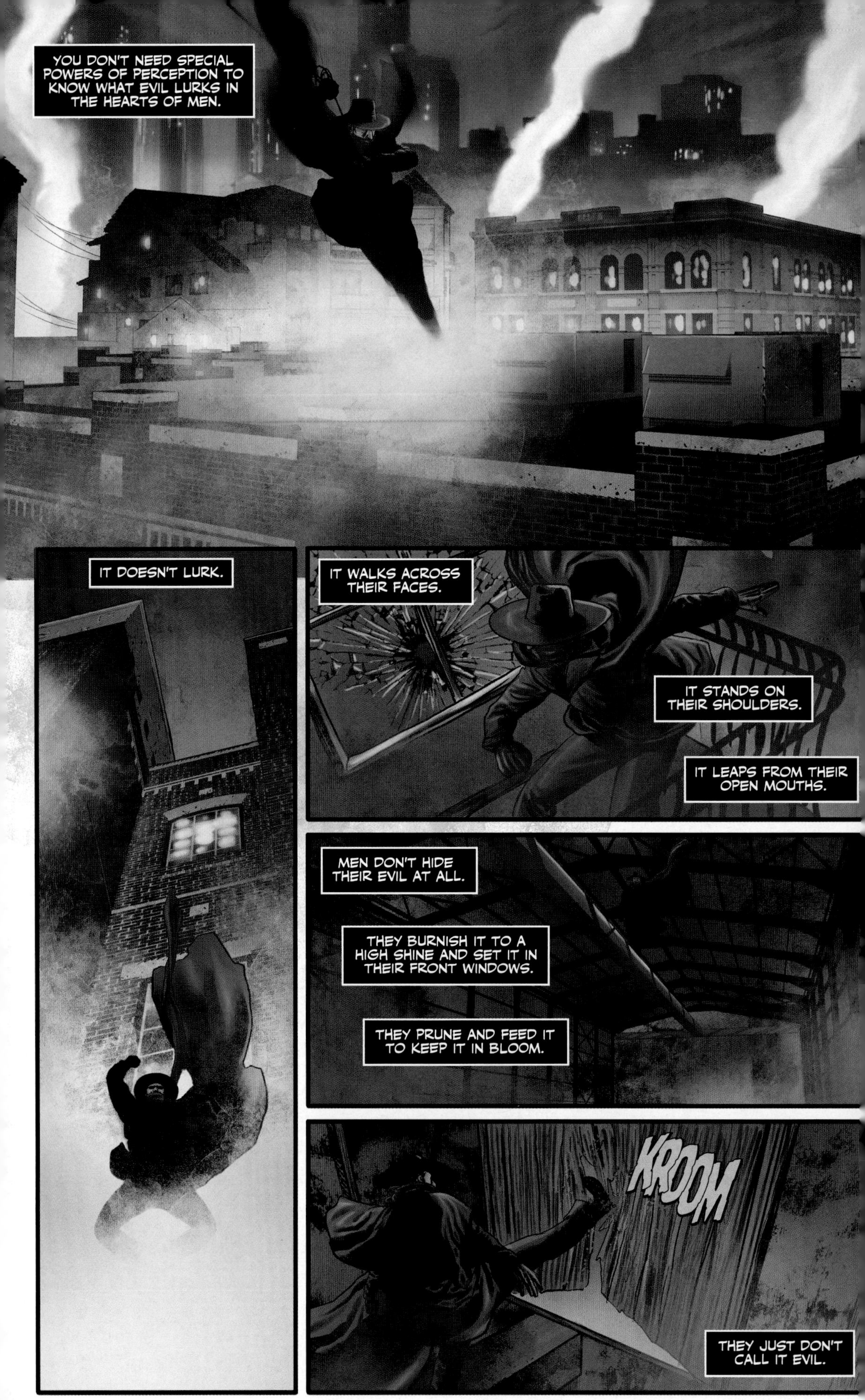
YOU DON'T NEED SPECIAL POWERS OF PERCEPTION TO KNOW WHAT EVIL LURKS IN THE HEARTS OF MEN.
IT DOESN'T LURK.
IT WALKS ACROSS THEIR FACES.
IT STANDS ON THEIR SHOULDERS.
IT LEAPS FROM THEIR OPEN MOUTHS.
MEN DON'T HIDE THEIR EVIL AT ALL.
THEY BURNISH IT TO A HIGH SHINE AND SET IT IN THEIR FRONT WINDOWS.
THEY PRUNE AND FEED IT TO KEEP IT IN BLOOM.
KROOM
THEY JUST DON'T CALL IT EVIL.

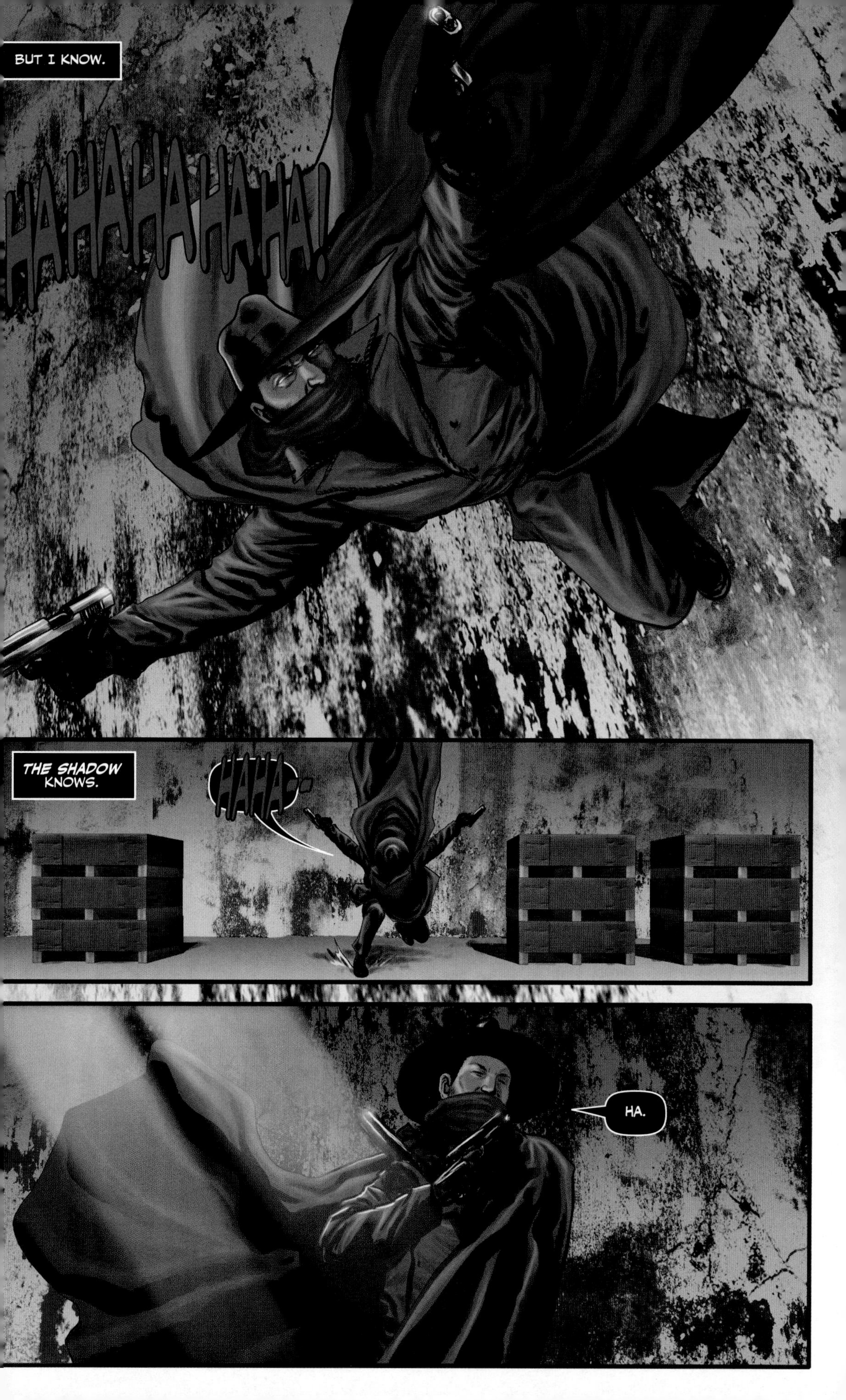
BUT I KNOW.
HAHAHAHAHA!
THE SHADOW KNOWS.
HAHA-
HA.

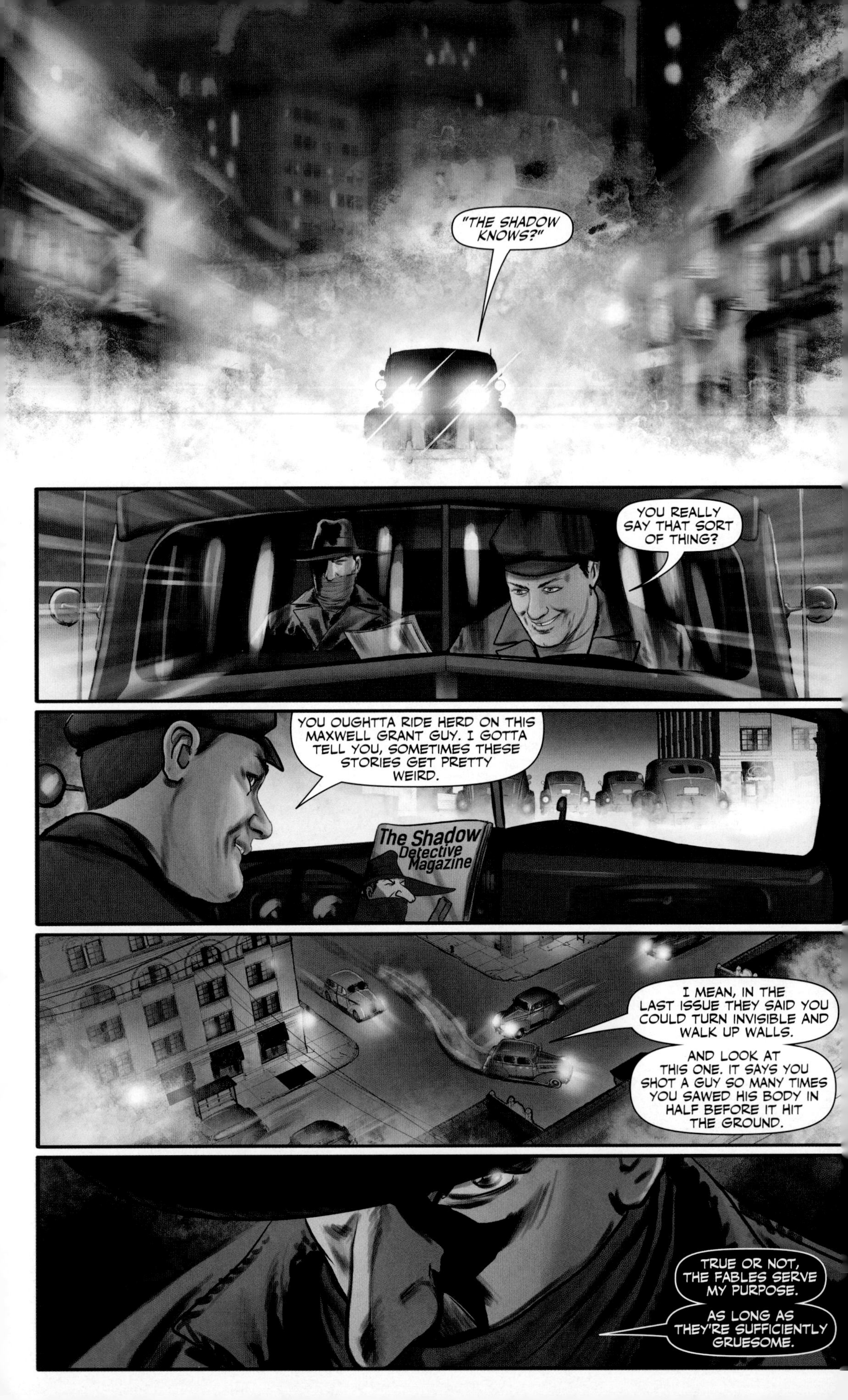
"THE SHADOW KNOWS?"
YOU REALLY SAY THAT SORT OF THING?
YOU OUGHTTA RIDE HERD ON THIS MAXWELL GRANT GUY. I GOTTA TELL YOU, SOMETIMES THESE STORIES GET PRETTY WEIRD.
The Shadow Detective Magazine
I MEAN, IN THE LAST ISSUE THEY SAID YOU COULD TURN INVISIBLE AND WALK UP WALLS.
AND LOOK AT THIS ONE. IT SAYS YOU SHOT A GUY SO MANY TIMES YOU SAWED HIS BODY IN HALF BEFORE IT HIT THE GROUND.
TRUE OR NOT, THE FABLES SERVE MY PURPOSE.
AS LONG AS THEY'RE SUFFICIENTLY GRUESOME.

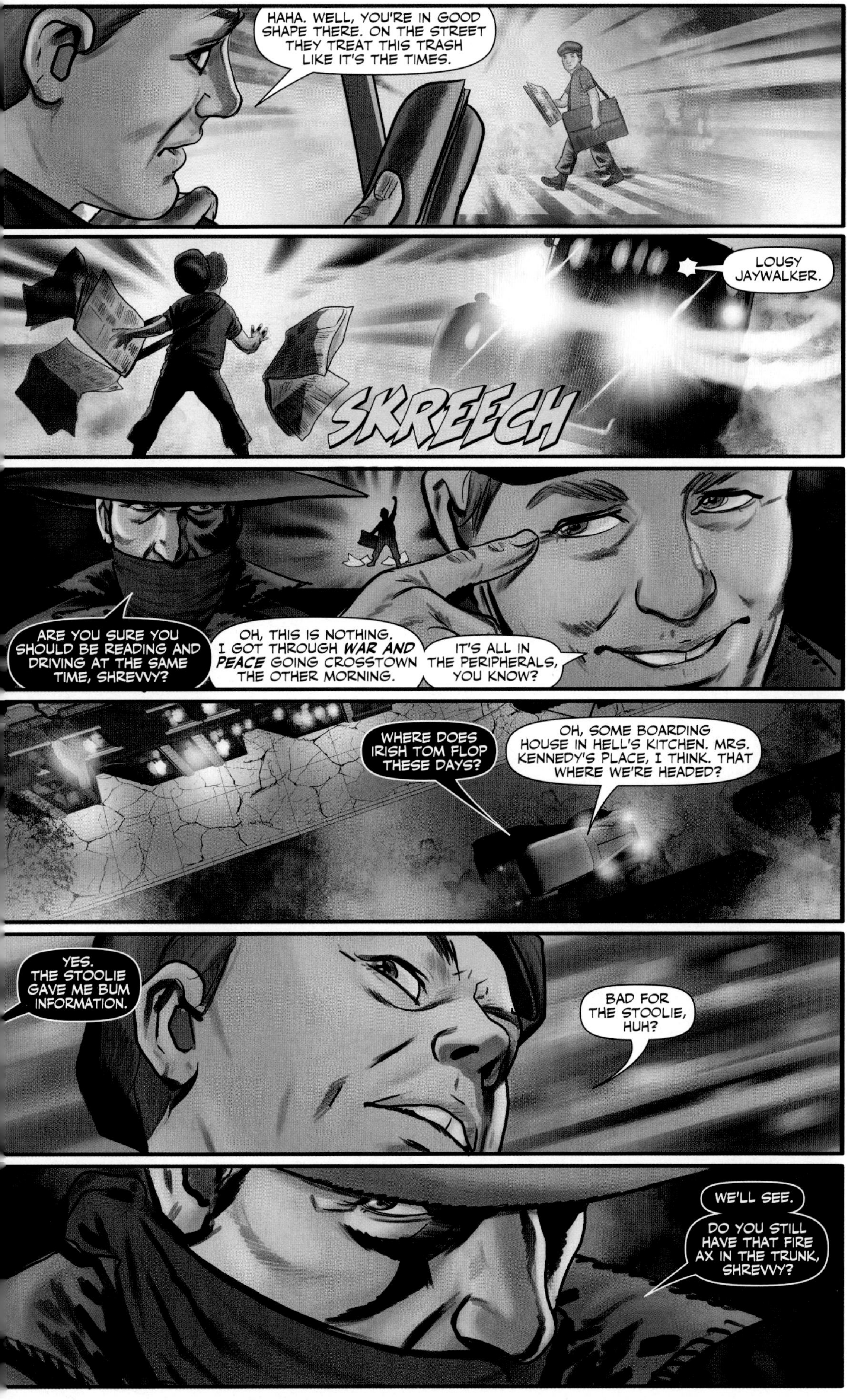
HAHA. WELL, YOU'RE IN GOOD SHAPE THERE. ON THE STREET THEY TREAT THIS TRASH LIKE IT'S THE TIMES.
LOUSY JAYWALKER.
SKREECH
ARE YOU SURE YOU SHOULD BE READING AND DRIVING AT THE SAME TIME, SHREVVY?
OH, THIS IS NOTHING. I GOT THROUGH WAR AND PEACE GOING CROSSTOWN THE OTHER MORNING.
IT'S ALL IN THE PERIPHERALS, YOU KNOW?
WHERE DOES IRISH TOM FLOP THESE DAYS?
OH, SOME BOARDING HOUSE IN HELL'S KITCHEN. MRS. KENNEDY'S PLACE, I THINK. THAT WHERE WE'RE HEADED?
YES. THE STOOLIE GAVE ME BUM INFORMATION.
BAD FOR THE STOOLIE, HUH?
WE'LL SEE.
DO YOU STILL HAVE THAT FIRE AX IN THE TRUNK, SHREVVY?

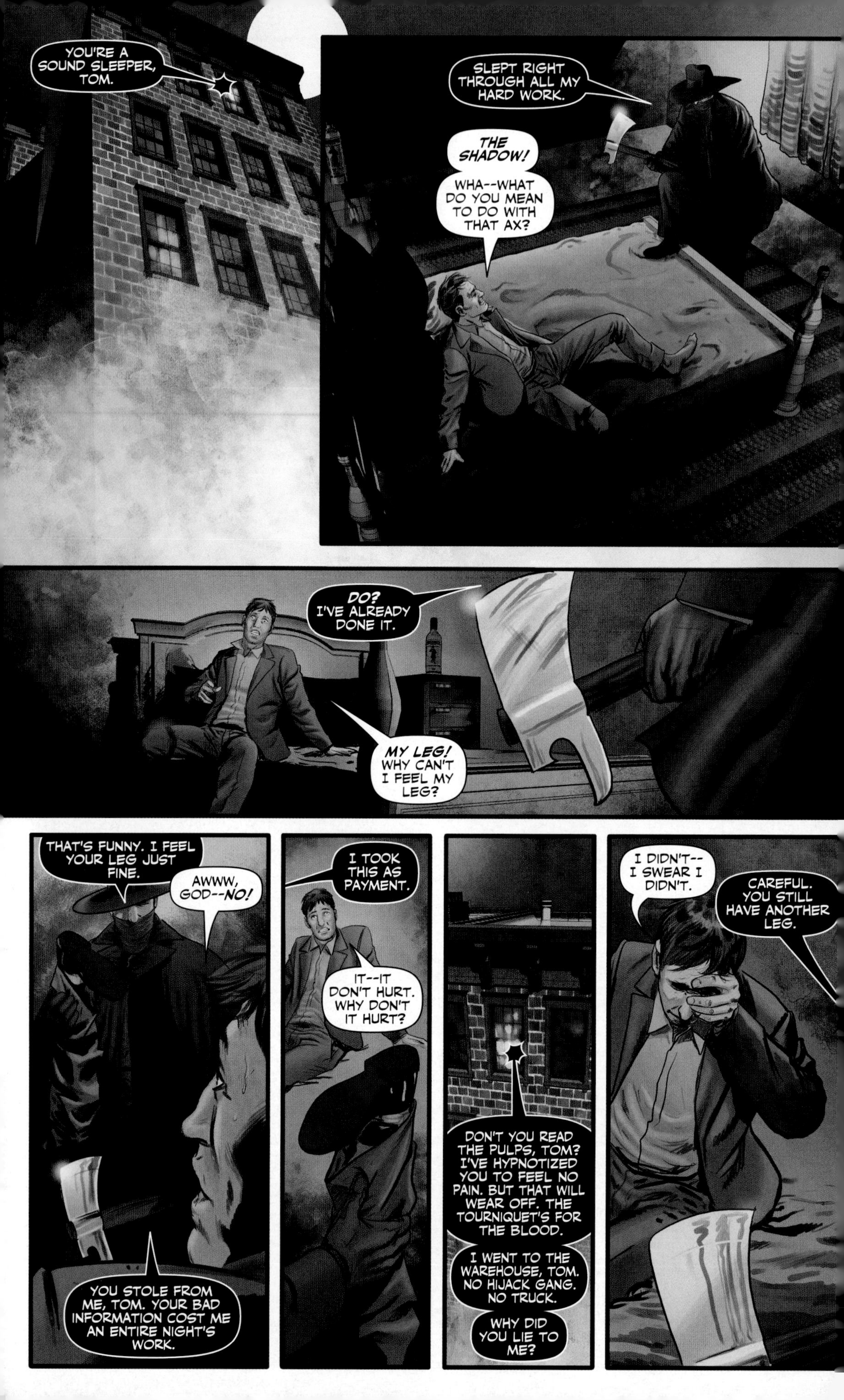
YOU'RE A SOUND SLEEPER, TOM.
SLEPT RIGHT THROUGH ALL MY HARD WORK.
THE SHADOW!
WHA--WHAT DO YOU MEAN TO DO WITH THAT AX?
DO? I'VE ALREADY DONE IT.
MY LEG! WHY CAN'T I FEEL MY LEG?
THAT'S FUNNY. I FEEL YOUR LEG JUST FINE.
AWWW, GOD--NO!
YOU STOLE FROM ME, TOM. YOUR BAD INFORMATION COST ME AN ENTIRE NIGHT'S WORK.
I TOOK THIS AS PAYMENT.
IT--IT DON'T HURT. WHY DON'T IT HURT?
DON'T YOU READ THE PULPS, TOM? I'VE HYPNOTIZED YOU TO FEEL NO PAIN. BUT THAT WILL WEAR OFF. THE TOURNIQUET'S FOR THE BLOOD.
I WENT TO THE WAREHOUSE, TOM. NO HIJACK GANG. NO TRUCK.
WHY DID YOU LIE TO ME?
I DIDN'T-- I SWEAR I DIDN'T.
CAREFUL. YOU STILL HAVE ANOTHER LEG.

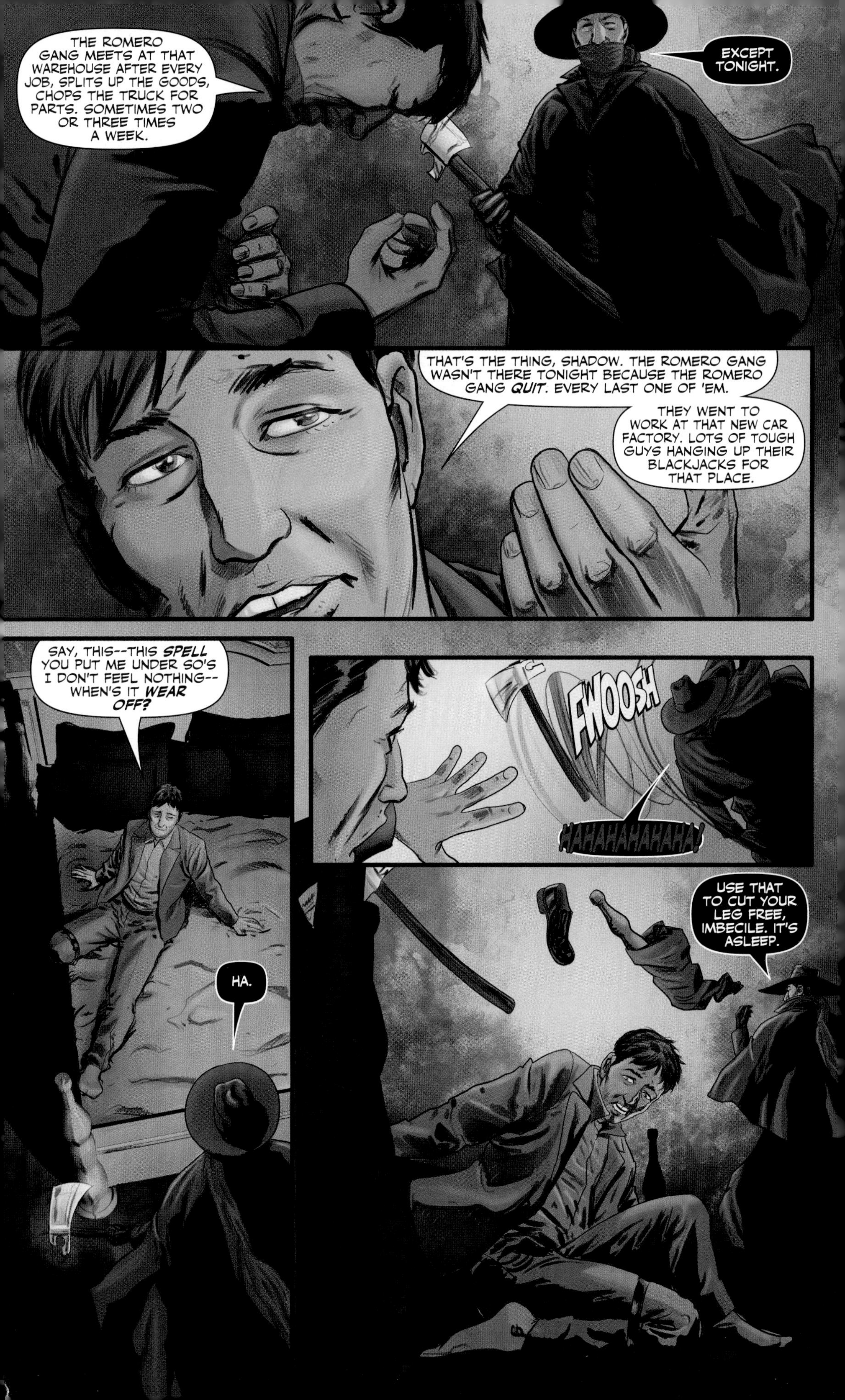
THE ROMERO GANG MEETS AT THAT WAREHOUSE AFTER EVERY JOB, SPLITS UP THE GOODS, CHOPS THE TRUCK FOR PARTS. SOMETIMES TWO OR THREE TIMES A WEEK.
EXCEPT TONIGHT.
THAT'S THE THING, SHADOW. THE ROMERO GANG WASN'T THERE TONIGHT BECAUSE THE ROMERO GANG QUIT. EVERY LAST ONE OF 'EM.
THEY WENT TO WORK AT THAT NEW CAR FACTORY. LOTS OF TOUGH GUYS HANGING UP THEIR BLACKJACKS FOR THAT PLACE.
SAY, THIS--THIS SPELL YOU PUT ME UNDER SO'S I DON'T FEEL NOTHING--WHEN'S IT WEAR OFF?
HA.
FWOOSH
HAHAHAHAHAHA!
USE THAT TO CUT YOUR LEG FREE, IMBECILE. IT'S ASLEEP.

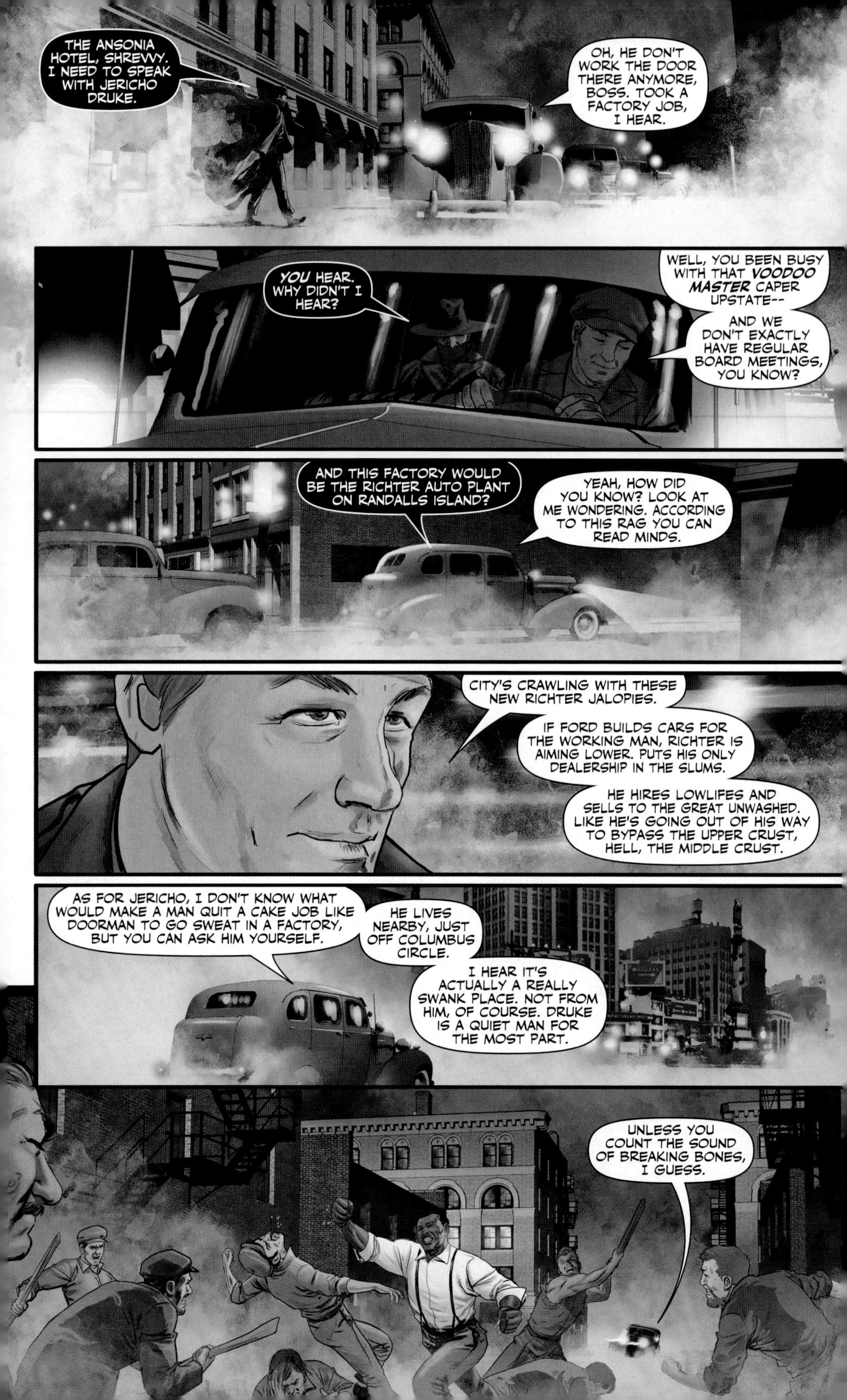
THE ANSONIA HOTEL, SHREVVY. I NEED TO SPEAK WITH JERICHO DRUKE.
OH, HE DON'T WORK THE DOOR THERE ANYMORE, BOSS. TOOK A FACTORY JOB, I HEAR.
YOU HEAR. WHY DIDN'T I HEAR?
WELL, YOU BEEN BUSY WITH THAT VOODOO MASTER CAPER UPSTATE--
AND WE DON'T EXACTLY HAVE REGULAR BOARD MEETINGS, YOU KNOW?
AND THIS FACTORY WOULD BE THE RICHTER AUTO PLANT ON RANDALLS ISLAND?
YEAH, HOW DID YOU KNOW? LOOK AT ME WONDERING. ACCORDING TO THIS RAG YOU CAN READ MINDS.
CITY'S CRAWLING WITH THESE NEW RICHTER JALOPIES.
IF FORD BUILDS CARS FOR THE WORKING MAN, RICHTER IS AIMING LOWER. PUTS HIS ONLY DEALERSHIP IN THE SLUMS.
HE HIRES LOWLIFES AND SELLS TO THE GREAT UNWASHED. LIKE HE'S GOING OUT OF HIS WAY TO BYPASS THE UPPER CRUST, HELL, THE MIDDLE CRUST.
AS FOR JERICHO, I DON'T KNOW WHAT WOULD MAKE A MAN QUIT A CAKE JOB LIKE DOORMAN TO GO SWEAT IN A FACTORY, BUT YOU CAN ASK HIM YOURSELF.
HE LIVES NEARBY, JUST OFF COLUMBUS CIRCLE.
I HEAR IT'S ACTUALLY A REALLY SWANK PLACE. NOT FROM HIM, OF COURSE. DRUKE IS A QUIET MAN FOR THE MOST PART.
UNLESS YOU COUNT THE SOUND OF BREAKING BONES, I GUESS.

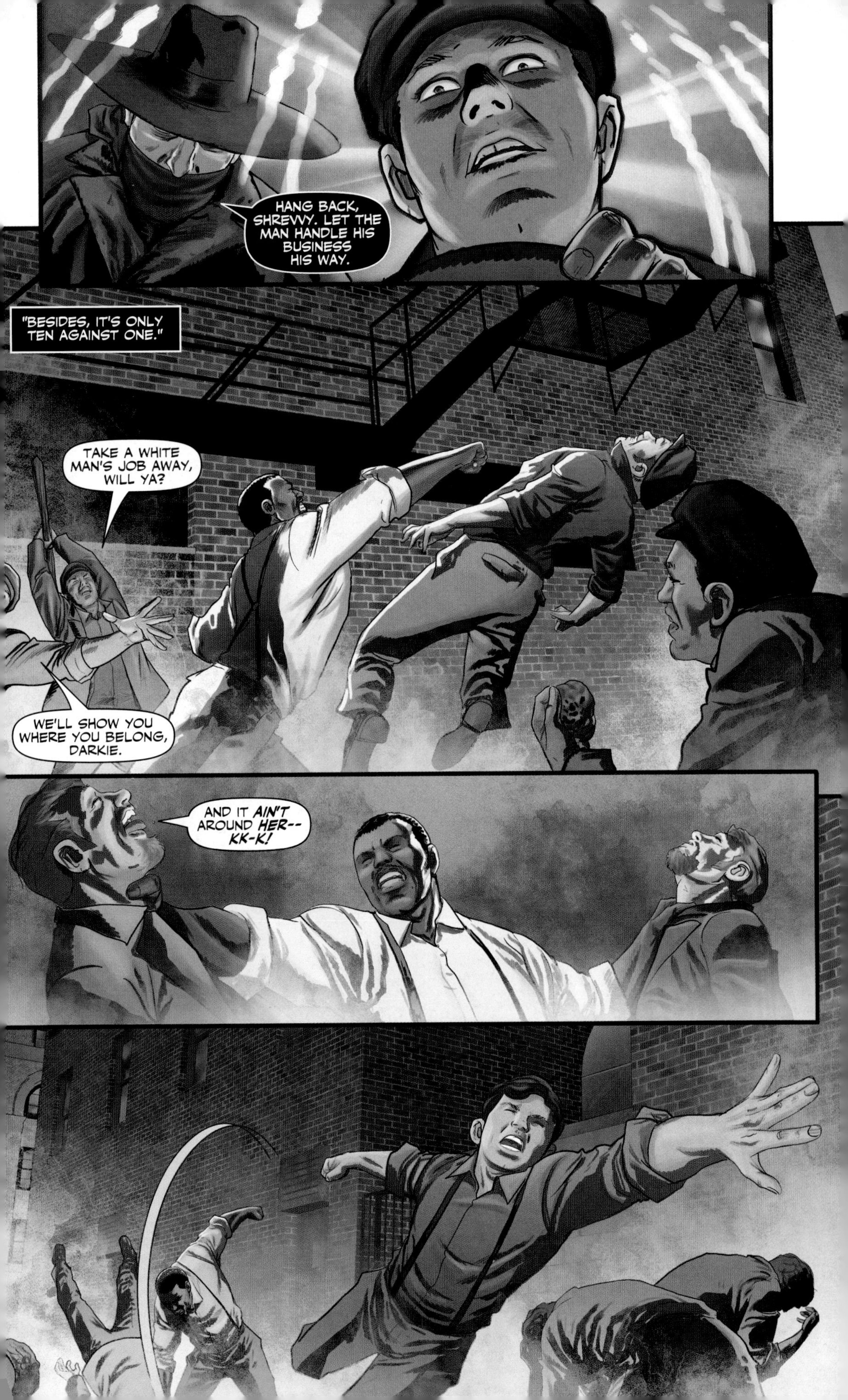

HANG BACK, SHREVVY. LET THE MAN HANDLE HIS BUSINESS HIS WAY.
"BESIDES, IT'S ONLY TEN AGAINST ONE."
TAKE A WHITE MAN'S JOB AWAY, WILL YA?
WE'LL SHOW YOU WHERE YOU BELONG, DARKIE.
AND IT AIN'T AROUND HER-- KK-K!

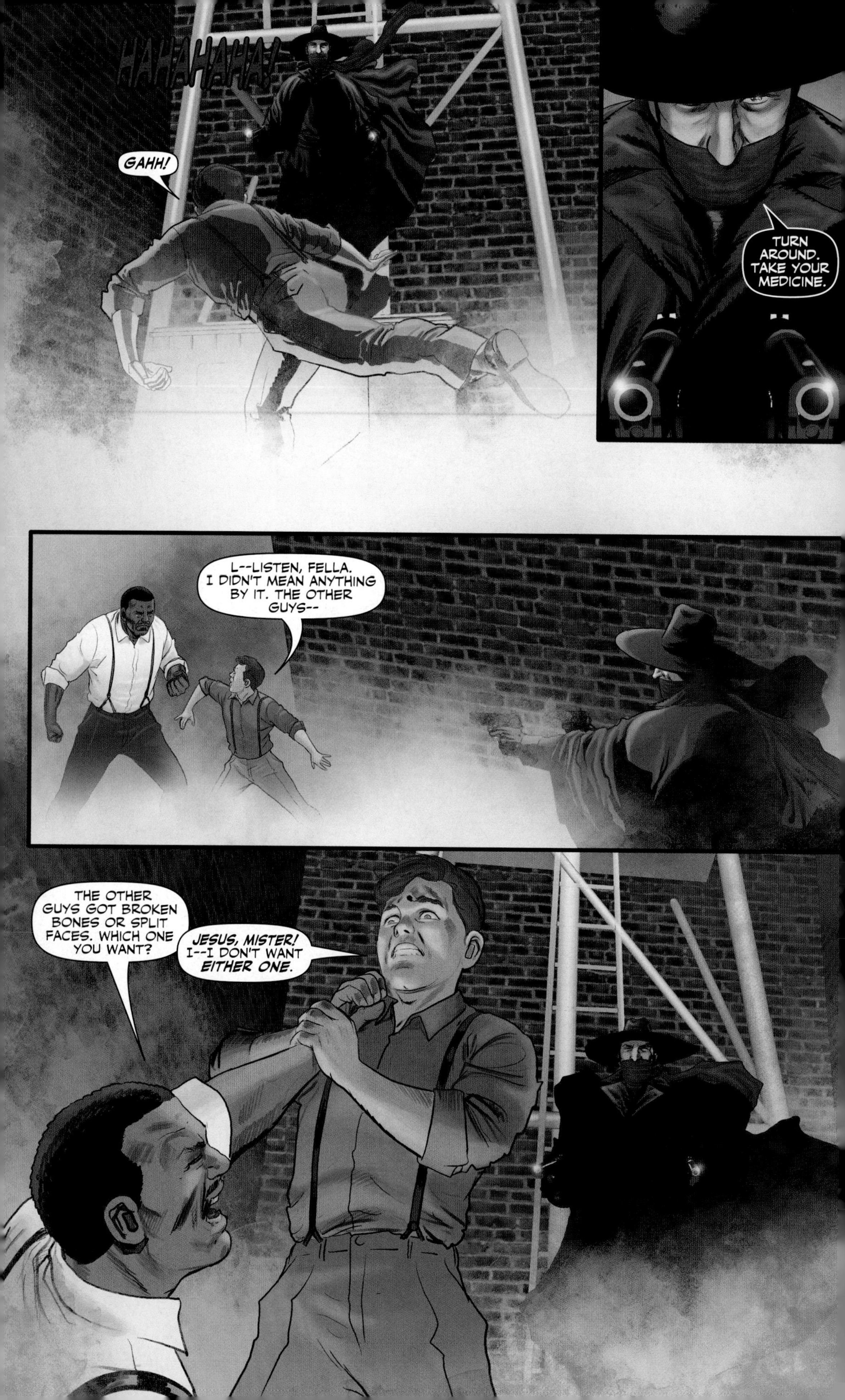
HAHAHAHA!
GAHH!
TURN AROUND. TAKE YOUR MEDICINE.
L--LISTEN, FELLA. I DIDN'T MEAN ANYTHING BY IT. THE OTHER GUYS--
THE OTHER GUYS GOT BROKEN BONES OR SPLIT FACES. WHICH ONE YOU WANT?
JESUS, MISTER! I--I DON'T WANT EITHER ONE.

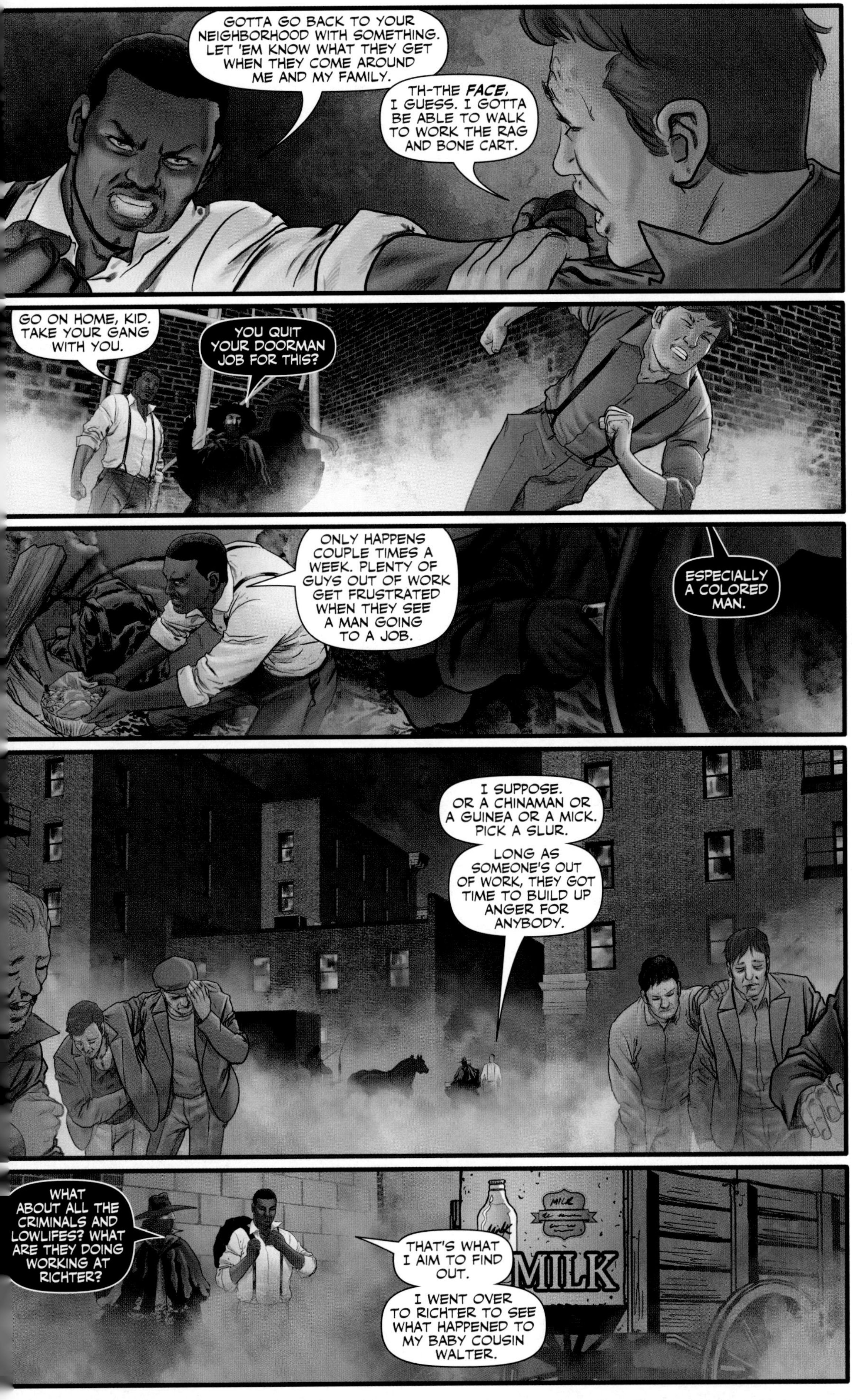
GOTTA GO BACK TO YOUR NEIGHBORHOOD WITH SOMETHING. LET 'EM KNOW WHAT THEY GET WHEN THEY COME AROUND ME AND MY FAMILY.
TH-THE *FACE*, I GUESS. I GOTTA BE ABLE TO WALK TO WORK THE RAG AND BONE CART.
GO ON HOME, KID. TAKE YOUR GANG WITH YOU.
YOU QUIT YOUR DOORMAN JOB FOR THIS?
ONLY HAPPENS COUPLE TIMES A WEEK. PLENTY OF GUYS OUT OF WORK GET FRUSTRATED WHEN THEY SEE A MAN GOING TO A JOB.
ESPECIALLY A COLORED MAN.
I SUPPOSE. OR A CHINAMAN OR A GUINEA OR A MICK. PICK A SLUR.
LONG AS SOMEONE'S OUT OF WORK, THEY GOT TIME TO BUILD UP ANGER FOR ANYBODY.
WHAT ABOUT ALL THE CRIMINALS AND LOWLIFES? WHAT ARE THEY DOING WORKING AT RICHTER?
THAT'S WHAT I AIM TO FIND OUT.
I WENT OVER TO RICHTER TO SEE WHAT HAPPENED TO MY BABY COUSIN WALTER.
MILK

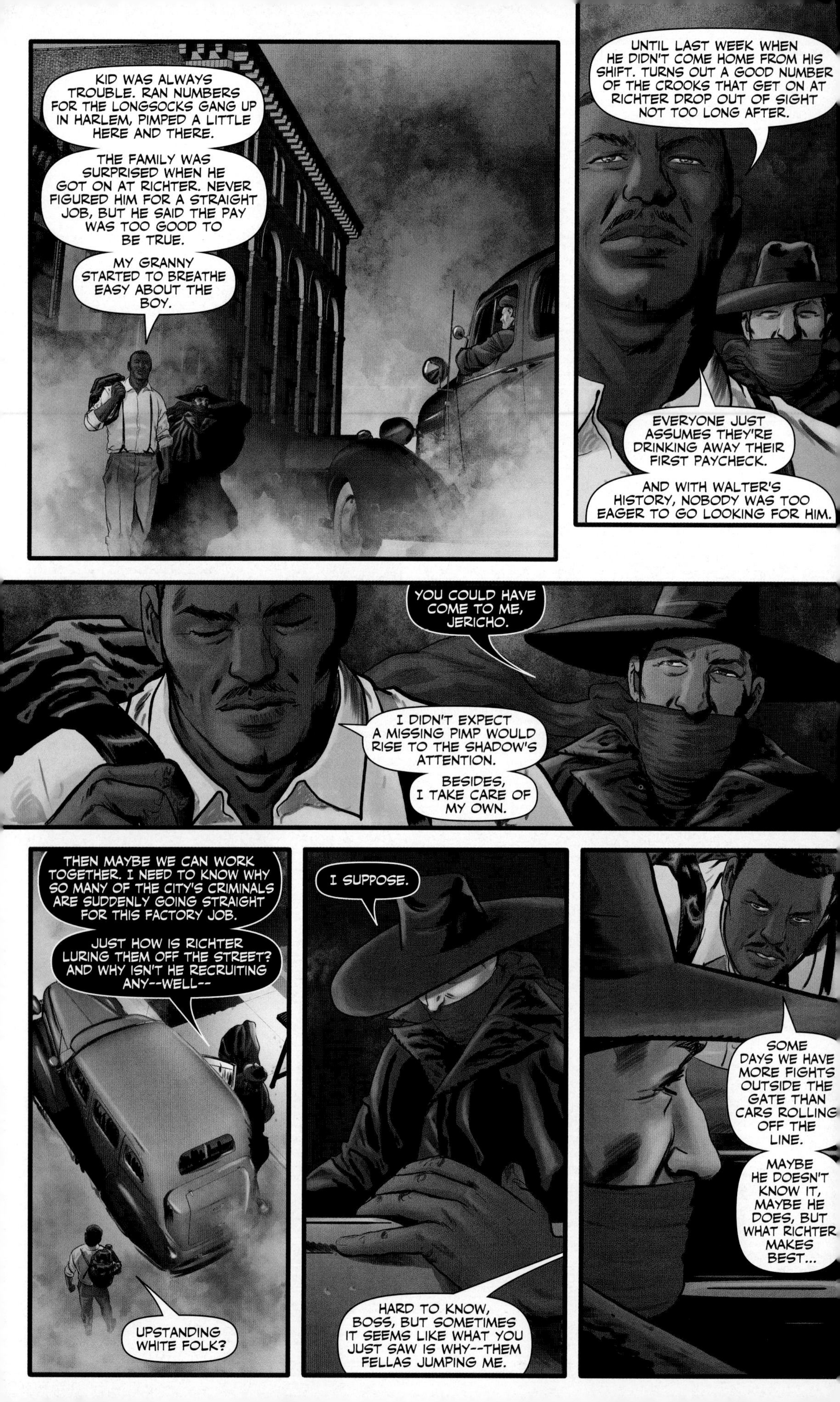
KID WAS ALWAYS TROUBLE. RAN NUMBERS FOR THE LONGSOCKS GANG UP IN HARLEM, PIMPED A LITTLE HERE AND THERE.
THE FAMILY WAS SURPRISED WHEN HE GOT ON AT RICHTER. NEVER FIGURED HIM FOR A STRAIGHT JOB, BUT HE SAID THE PAY WAS TOO GOOD TO BE TRUE.
MY GRANNY STARTED TO BREATHE EASY ABOUT THE BOY.
UNTIL LAST WEEK WHEN HE DIDN'T COME HOME FROM HIS SHIFT. TURNS OUT A GOOD NUMBER OF THE CROOKS THAT GET ON AT RICHTER DROP OUT OF SIGHT NOT TOO LONG AFTER.
EVERYONE JUST ASSUMES THEY'RE DRINKING AWAY THEIR FIRST PAYCHECK.
AND WITH WALTER'S HISTORY, NOBODY WAS TOO EAGER TO GO LOOKING FOR HIM.
YOU COULD HAVE COME TO ME, JERICHO.
I DIDN'T EXPECT A MISSING PIMP WOULD RISE TO THE SHADOW'S ATTENTION.
BESIDES, I TAKE CARE OF MY OWN.
THEN MAYBE WE CAN WORK TOGETHER. I NEED TO KNOW WHY SO MANY OF THE CITY'S CRIMINALS ARE SUDDENLY GOING STRAIGHT FOR THIS FACTORY JOB.
JUST HOW IS RICHTER LURING THEM OFF THE STREET? AND WHY ISN'T HE RECRUITING ANY--WELL--
UPSTANDING WHITE FOLK?
I SUPPOSE.
HARD TO KNOW, BOSS, BUT SOMETIMES IT SEEMS LIKE WHAT YOU JUST SAW IS WHY--THEM FELLAS JUMPING ME.
SOME DAYS WE HAVE MORE FIGHTS OUTSIDE THE GATE THAN CARS ROLLING OFF THE LINE.
MAYBE HE DOESN'T KNOW IT, MAYBE HE DOES, BUT WHAT RICHTER MAKES BEST...

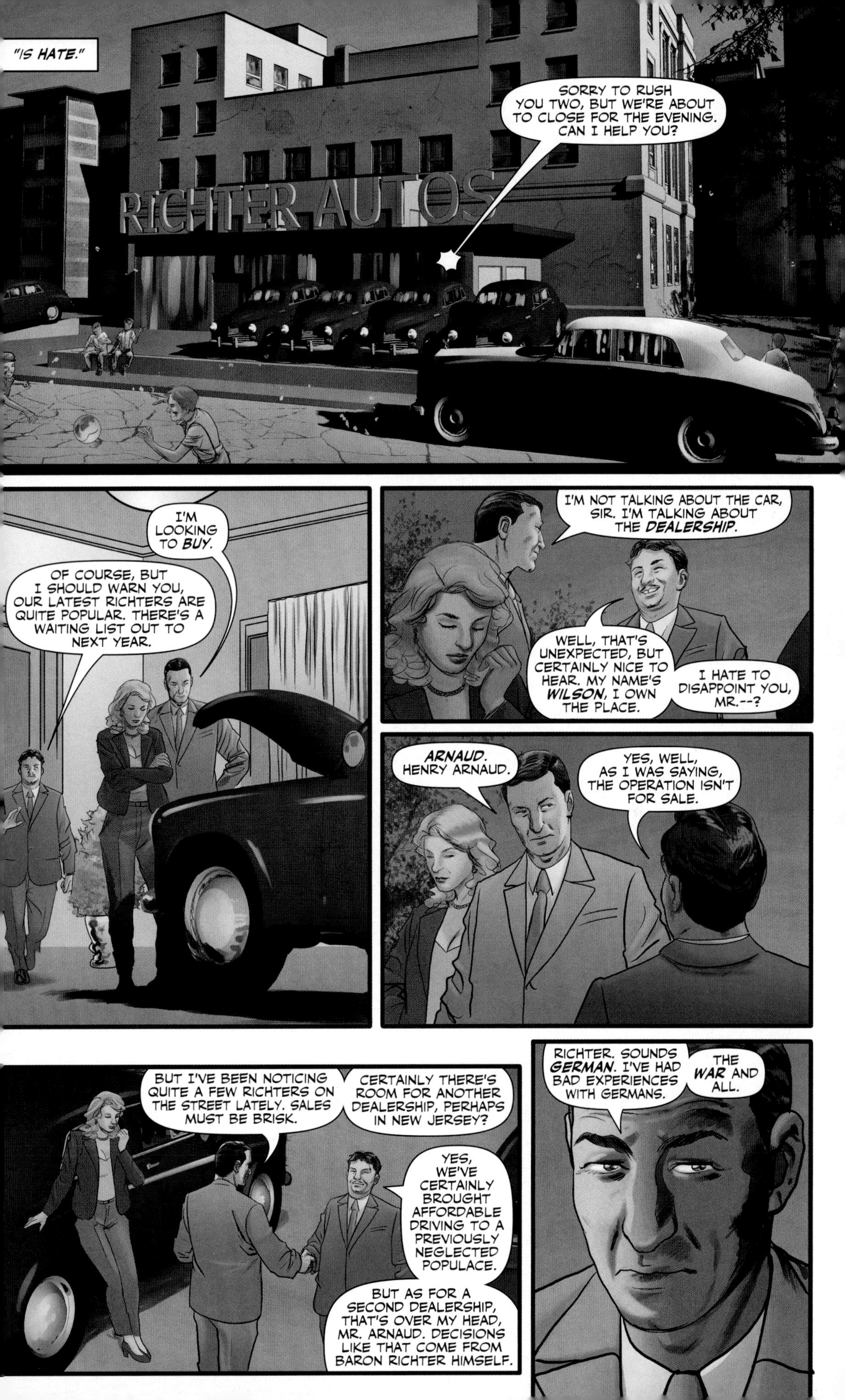
"IS HATE."
SORRY TO RUSH YOU TWO, BUT WE'RE ABOUT TO CLOSE FOR THE EVENING. CAN I HELP YOU?
RICHTER AUTOS
I'M LOOKING TO BUY.
OF COURSE, BUT I SHOULD WARN YOU, OUR LATEST RICHTERS ARE QUITE POPULAR. THERE'S A WAITING LIST OUT TO NEXT YEAR.
I'M NOT TALKING ABOUT THE CAR, SIR. I'M TALKING ABOUT THE DEALERSHIP.
WELL, THAT'S UNEXPECTED, BUT CERTAINLY NICE TO HEAR. MY NAME'S WILSON, I OWN THE PLACE.
I HATE TO DISAPPOINT YOU, MR.--?
ARNAUD. HENRY ARNAUD.
YES, WELL, AS I WAS SAYING, THE OPERATION ISN'T FOR SALE.
BUT I'VE BEEN NOTICING QUITE A FEW RICHTERS ON THE STREET LATELY. SALES MUST BE BRISK.
CERTAINLY THERE'S ROOM FOR ANOTHER DEALERSHIP, PERHAPS IN NEW JERSEY?
YES, WE'VE CERTAINLY BROUGHT AFFORDABLE DRIVING TO A PREVIOUSLY NEGLECTED POPULACE.
BUT AS FOR A SECOND DEALERSHIP, THAT'S OVER MY HEAD, MR. ARNAUD. DECISIONS LIKE THAT COME FROM BARON RICHTER HIMSELF.
RICHTER. SOUNDS GERMAN. I'VE HAD BAD EXPERIENCES WITH GERMANS.
THE WAR AND ALL.

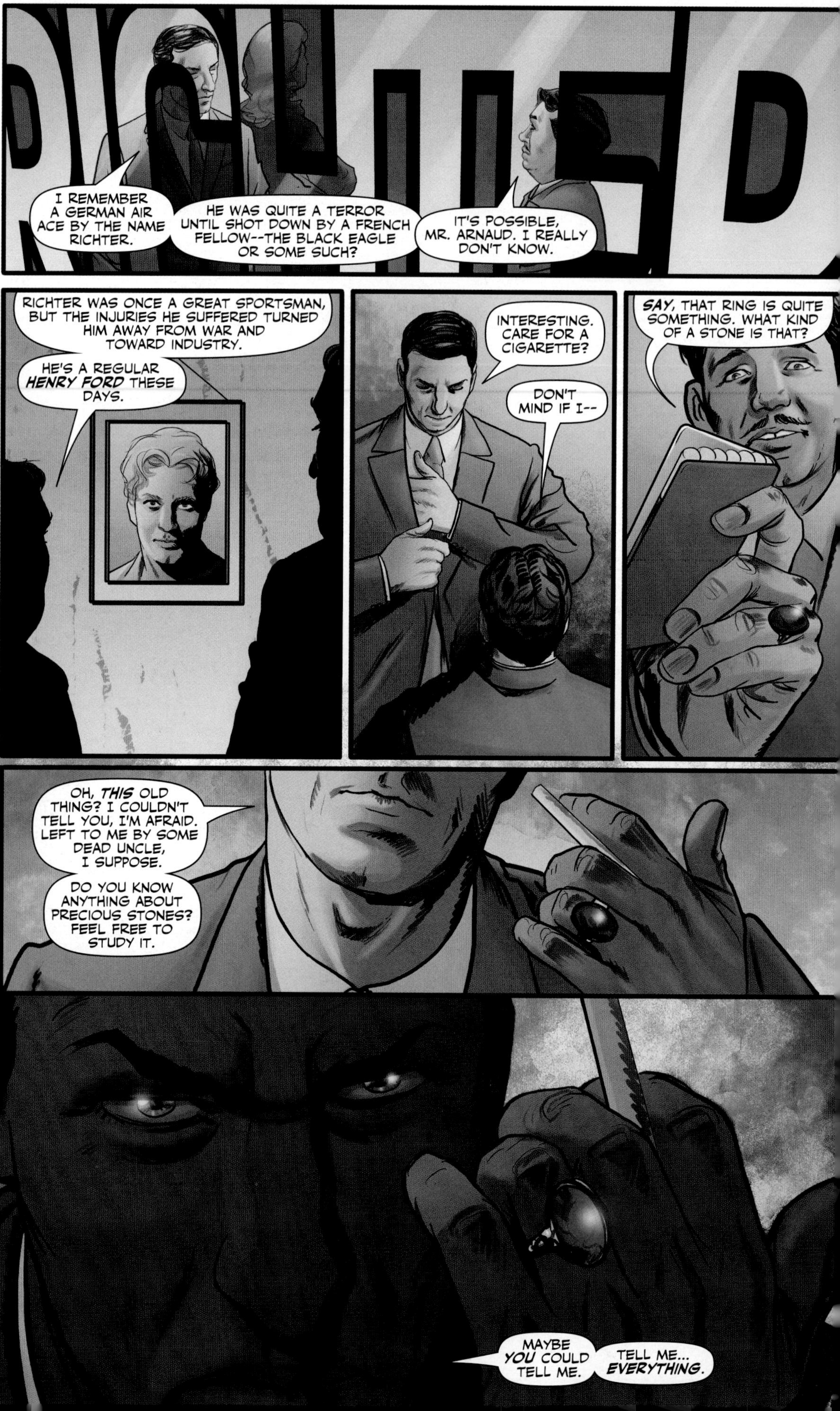

I REMEMBER A GERMAN AIR ACE BY THE NAME RICHTER.
HE WAS QUITE A TERROR UNTIL SHOT DOWN BY A FRENCH FELLOW--THE BLACK EAGLE OR SOME SUCH?
IT'S POSSIBLE, MR. ARNAUD. I REALLY DON'T KNOW.
RICHTER WAS ONCE A GREAT SPORTSMAN, BUT THE INJURIES HE SUFFERED TURNED HIM AWAY FROM WAR AND TOWARD INDUSTRY.
HE'S A REGULAR ***HENRY FORD*** THESE DAYS.
INTERESTING. CARE FOR A CIGARETTE?
DON'T MIND IF I--
SAY, THAT RING IS QUITE SOMETHING. WHAT KIND OF A STONE IS THAT?
OH, ***THIS*** OLD THING? I COULDN'T TELL YOU, I'M AFRAID. LEFT TO ME BY SOME DEAD UNCLE, I SUPPOSE.
DO YOU KNOW ANYTHING ABOUT PRECIOUS STONES? FEEL FREE TO STUDY IT.
MAYBE ***YOU*** COULD TELL ME.
TELL ME... ***EVERYTHING***.

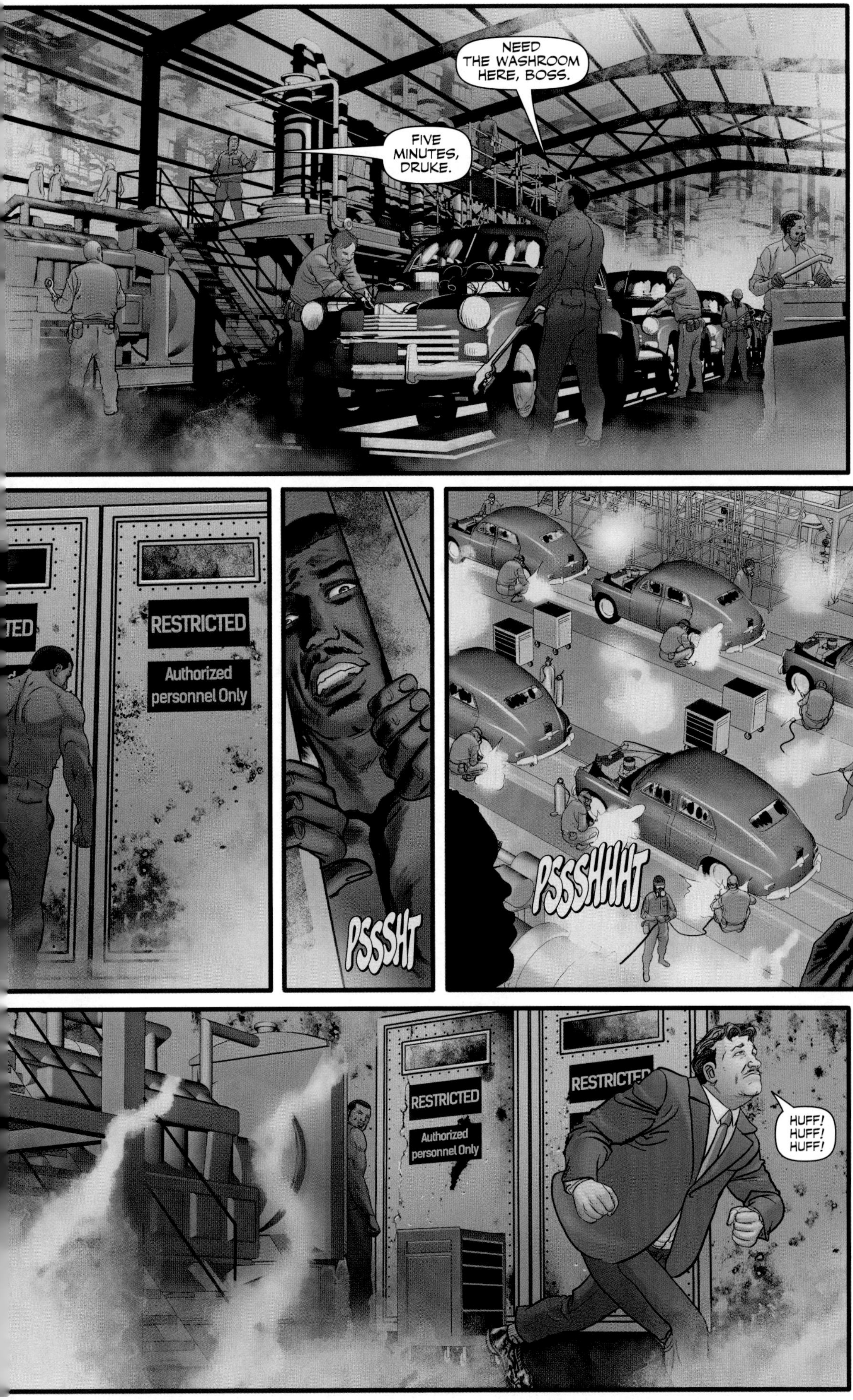

NEED THE WASHROOM HERE, BOSS.
FIVE MINUTES, DRUKE.
RESTRICTED
Authorized personnel Only
PSSSHT
PSSSHHHT
RESTRICTED
Authorized personnel Only
HUFF! HUFF! HUFF!

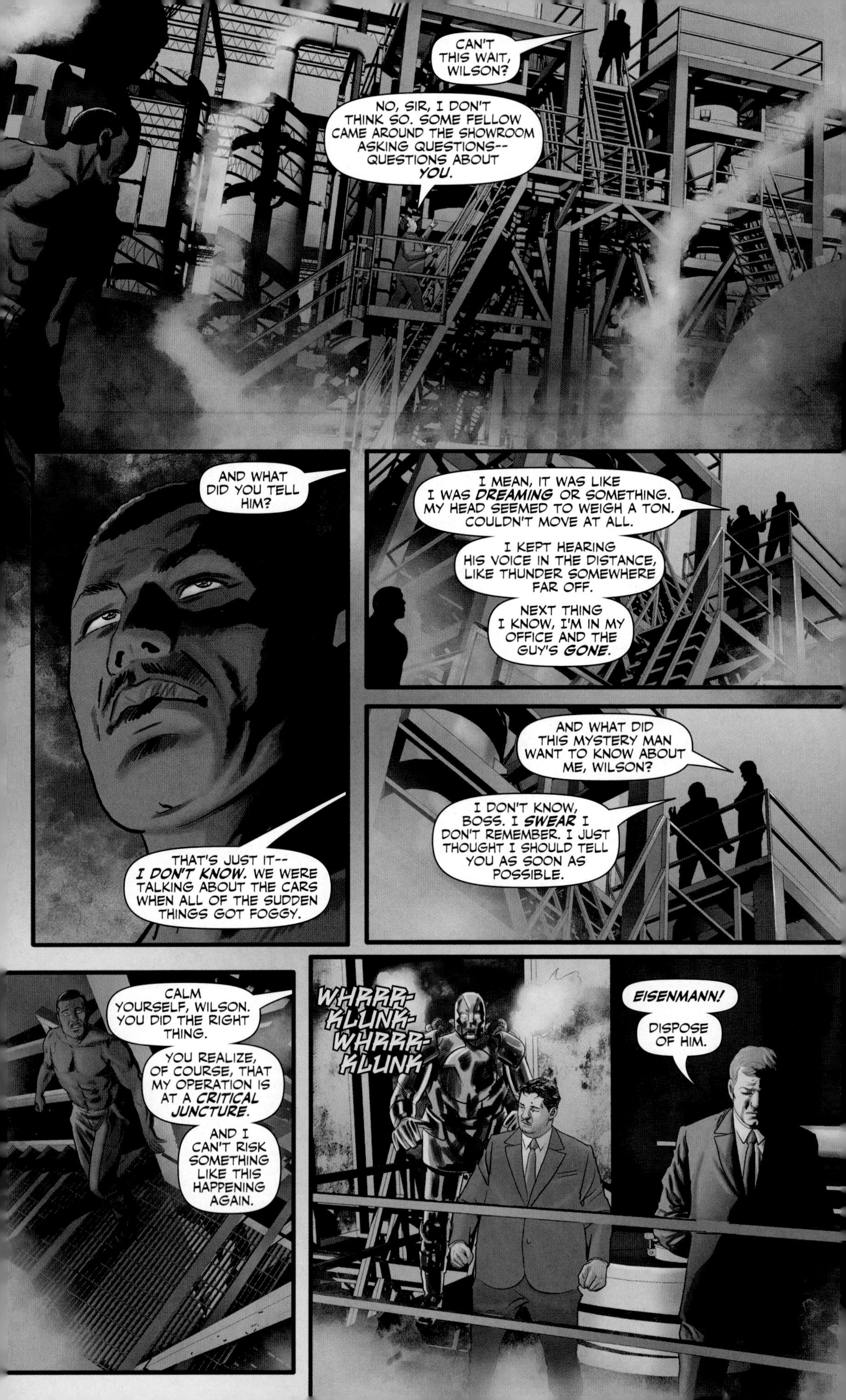
CAN'T THIS WAIT, WILSON?
NO, SIR, I DON'T THINK SO. SOME FELLOW CAME AROUND THE SHOWROOM ASKING QUESTIONS-- QUESTIONS ABOUT YOU.
AND WHAT DID YOU TELL HIM?
THAT'S JUST IT-- I DON'T KNOW. WE WERE TALKING ABOUT THE CARS WHEN ALL OF THE SUDDEN THINGS GOT FOGGY.
I MEAN, IT WAS LIKE I WAS DREAMING OR SOMETHING. MY HEAD SEEMED TO WEIGH A TON. COULDN'T MOVE AT ALL.
I KEPT HEARING HIS VOICE IN THE DISTANCE, LIKE THUNDER SOMEWHERE FAR OFF.
NEXT THING I KNOW, I'M IN MY OFFICE AND THE GUY'S GONE.
AND WHAT DID THIS MYSTERY MAN WANT TO KNOW ABOUT ME, WILSON?
I DON'T KNOW, BOSS. I SWEAR I DON'T REMEMBER. I JUST THOUGHT I SHOULD TELL YOU AS SOON AS POSSIBLE.
CALM YOURSELF, WILSON. YOU DID THE RIGHT THING.
YOU REALIZE, OF COURSE, THAT MY OPERATION IS AT A CRITICAL JUNCTURE.
AND I CAN'T RISK SOMETHING LIKE THIS HAPPENING AGAIN.
WHRRR-KLUNK-WHRRR-KLUNK
EISENMANN!
DISPOSE OF HIM.

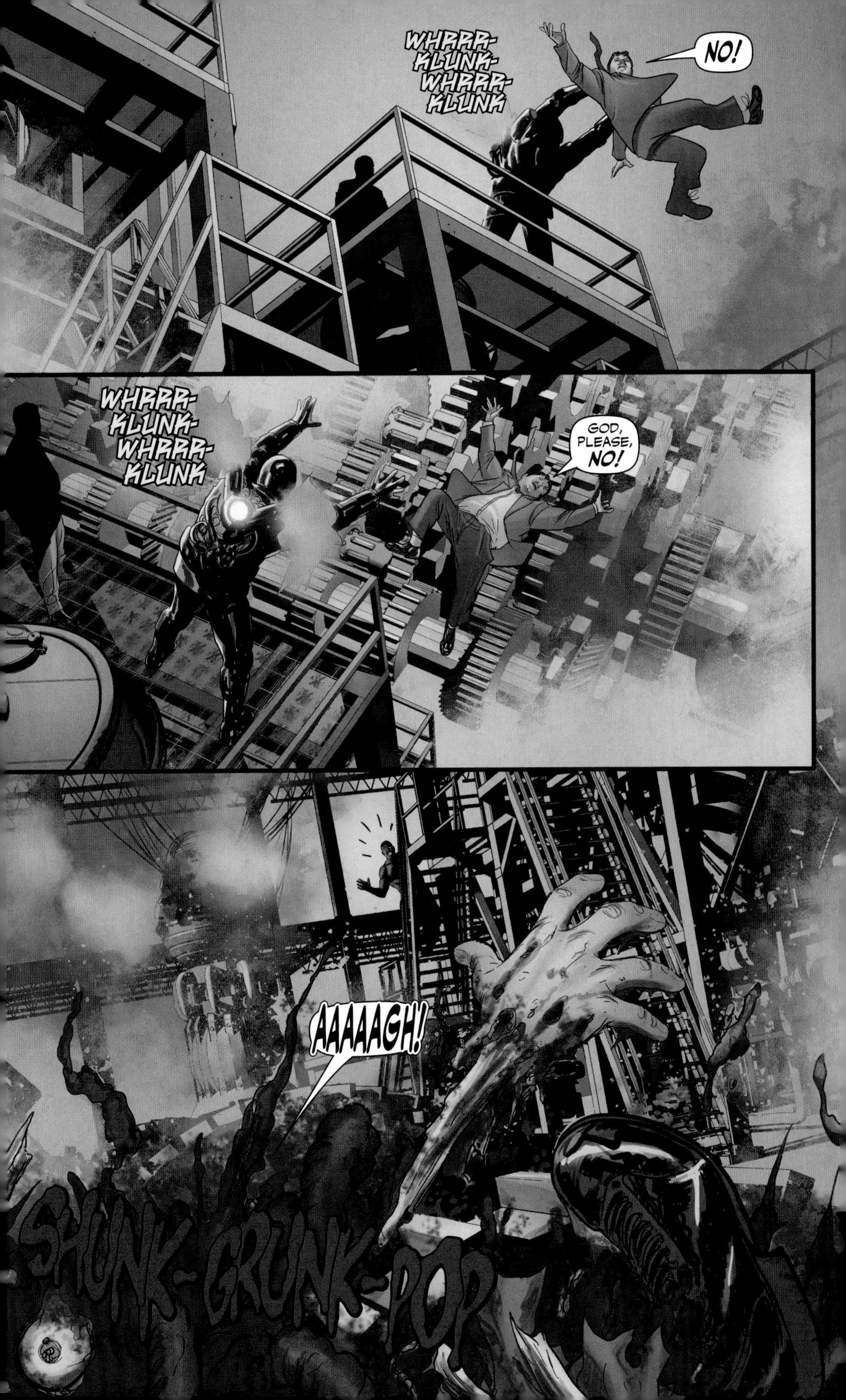
WHRRR-KLUNK-WHRRR-KLUNK
NO!
WHRRR-KLUNK-WHRRR-KLUNK
GOD, PLEASE, NO!
AAAAAGH!
SHUNK-GRUNK-POP

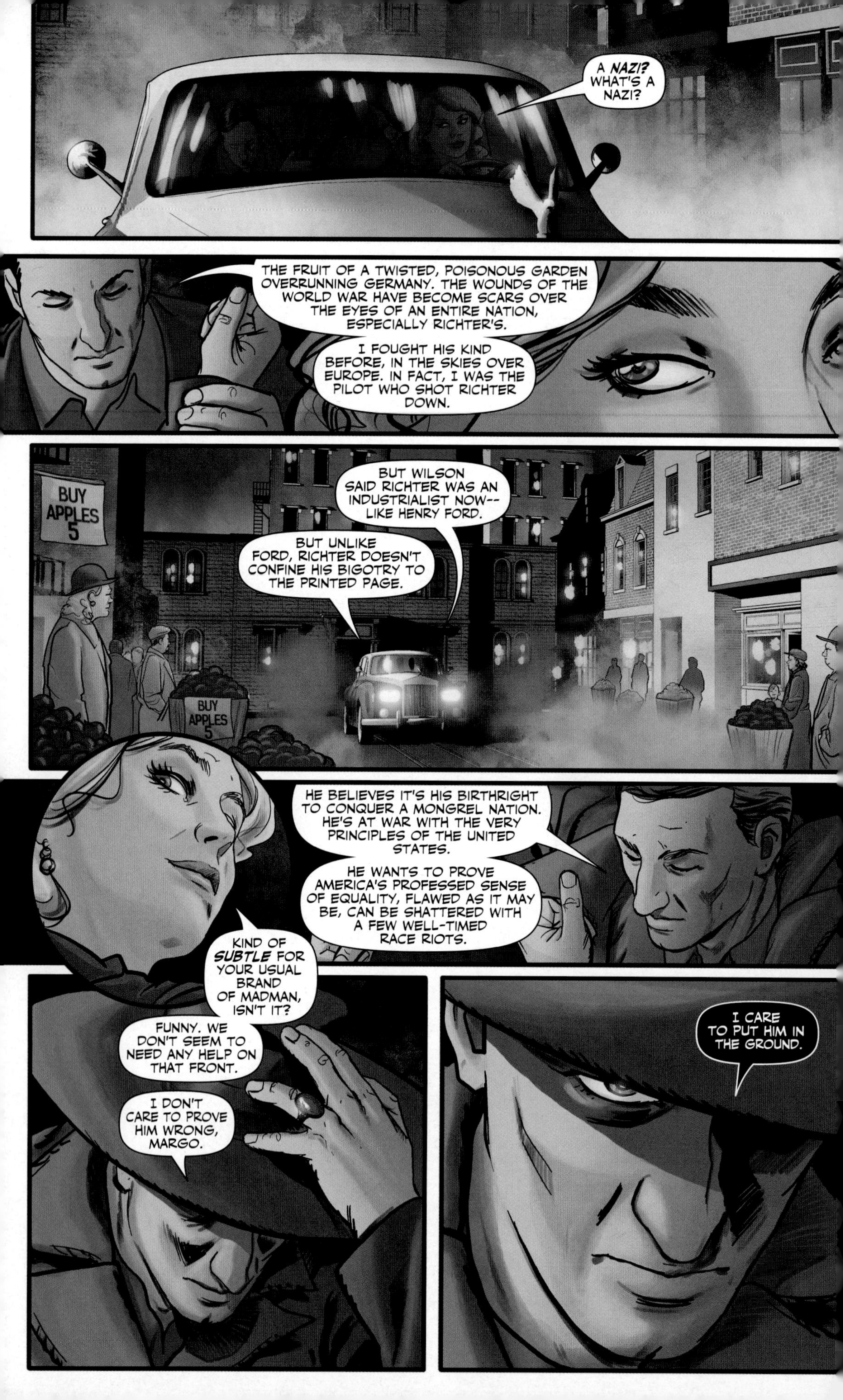
A *NAZI?* WHAT'S A NAZI?
THE FRUIT OF A TWISTED, POISONOUS GARDEN OVERRUNNING GERMANY. THE WOUNDS OF THE WORLD WAR HAVE BECOME SCARS OVER THE EYES OF AN ENTIRE NATION, ESPECIALLY RICHTER'S.
I FOUGHT HIS KIND BEFORE, IN THE SKIES OVER EUROPE. IN FACT, I WAS THE PILOT WHO SHOT RICHTER DOWN.
BUY APPLES 5
BUT WILSON SAID RICHTER WAS AN INDUSTRIALIST NOW-- LIKE HENRY FORD.
BUT UNLIKE FORD, RICHTER DOESN'T CONFINE HIS BIGOTRY TO THE PRINTED PAGE.
BUY APPLES 5
HE BELIEVES IT'S HIS BIRTHRIGHT TO CONQUER A MONGREL NATION. HE'S AT WAR WITH THE VERY PRINCIPLES OF THE UNITED STATES.
HE WANTS TO PROVE AMERICA'S PROFESSED SENSE OF EQUALITY, FLAWED AS IT MAY BE, CAN BE SHATTERED WITH A FEW WELL-TIMED RACE RIOTS.
KIND OF *SUBTLE* FOR YOUR USUAL BRAND OF MADMAN, ISN'T IT?
FUNNY. WE DON'T SEEM TO NEED ANY HELP ON THAT FRONT.
I DON'T CARE TO PROVE HIM WRONG, MARGO.
I CARE TO PUT HIM IN THE GROUND.

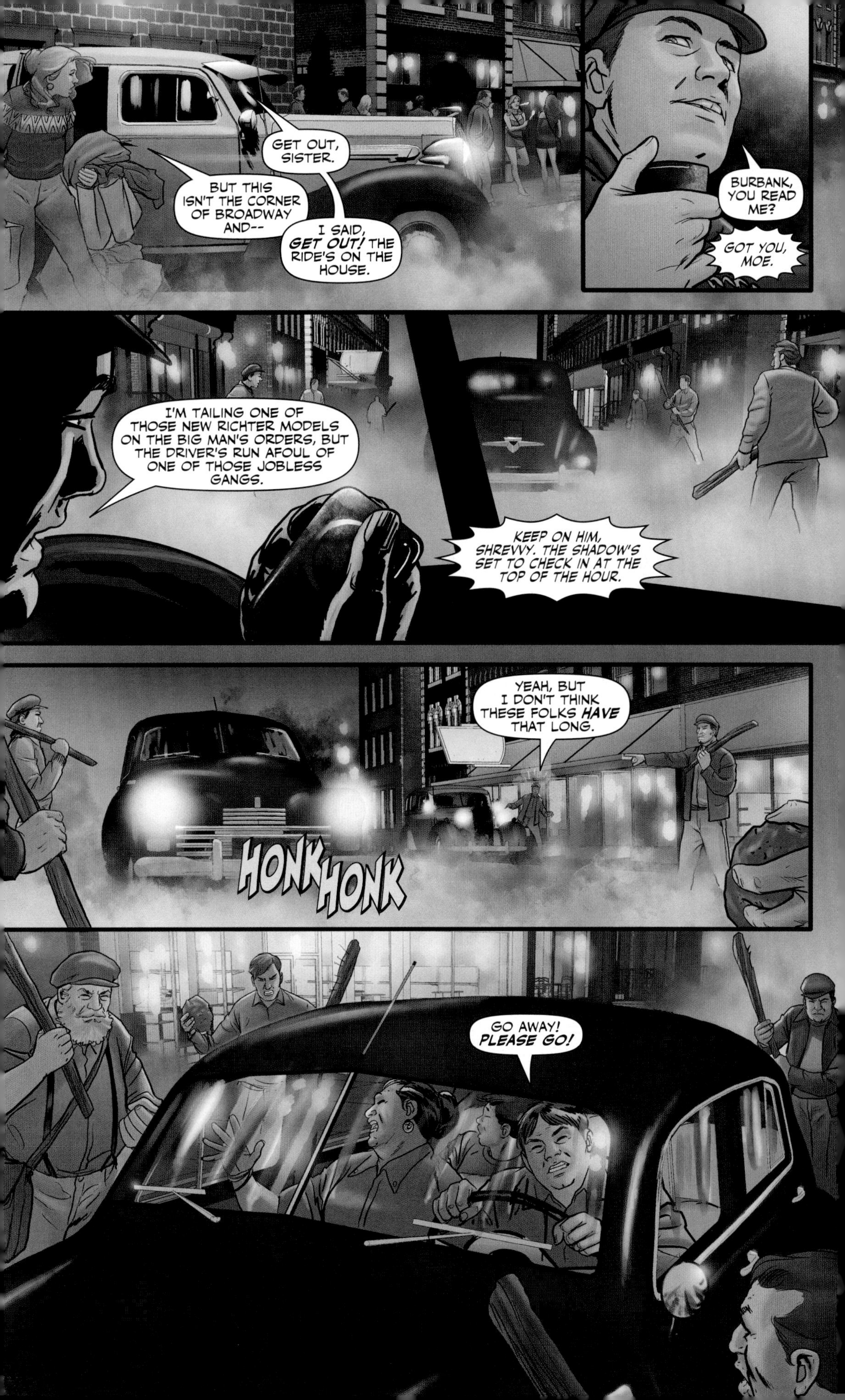
GET OUT, SISTER.
BUT THIS ISN'T THE CORNER OF BROADWAY AND--
I SAID, **GET OUT!** THE RIDE'S ON THE HOUSE.
BURBANK, YOU READ ME?
GOT YOU, MOE.
I'M TAILING ONE OF THOSE NEW RICHTER MODELS ON THE BIG MAN'S ORDERS, BUT THE DRIVER'S RUN AFOUL OF ONE OF THOSE JOBLESS GANGS.
KEEP ON HIM, SHREVVY. THE SHADOW'S SET TO CHECK IN AT THE TOP OF THE HOUR.
YEAH, BUT I DON'T THINK THESE FOLKS **HAVE** THAT LONG.
HONK HONK
GO AWAY! **PLEASE GO!**

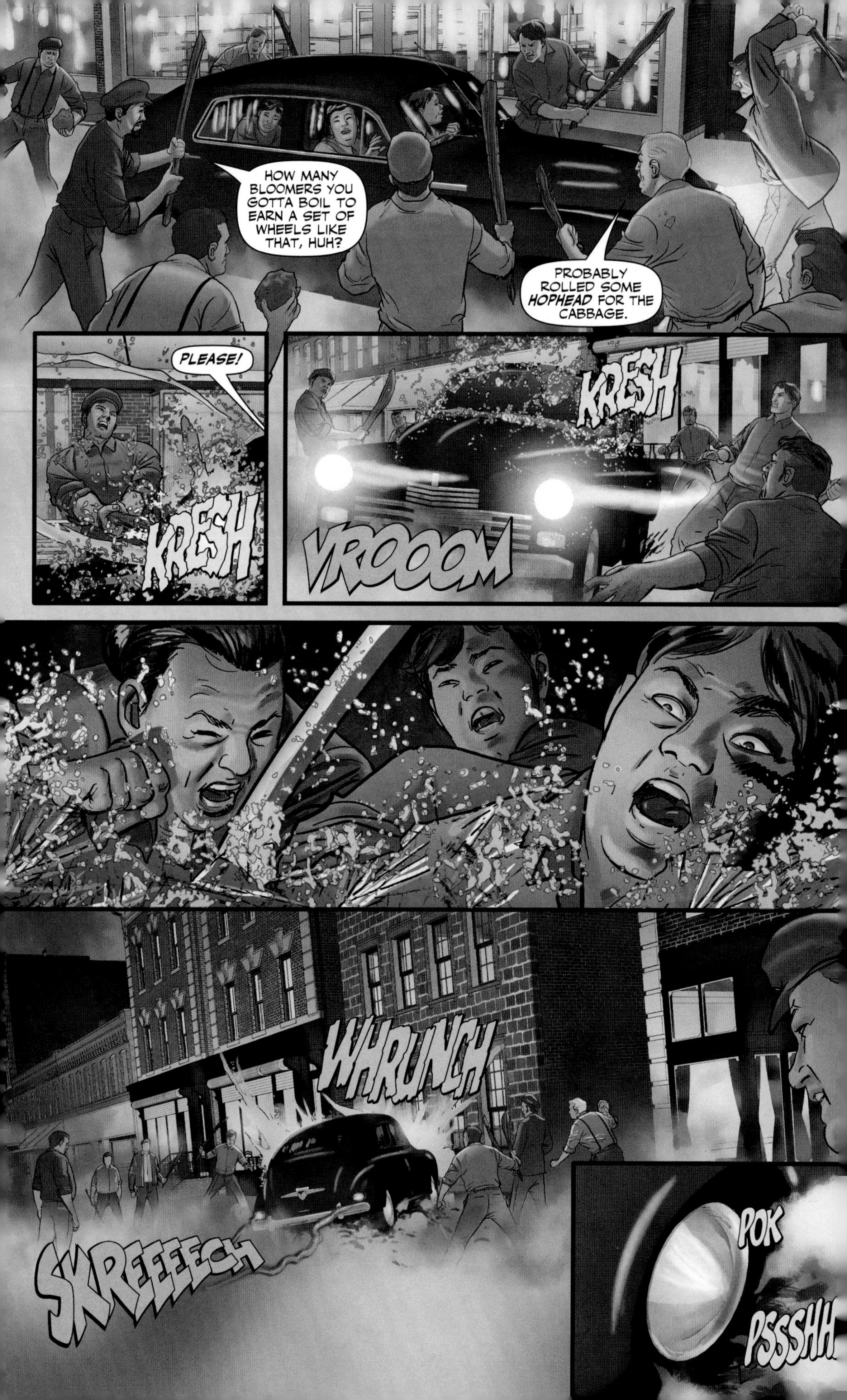

HOW MANY BLOOMERS YOU GOTTA BOIL TO EARN A SET OF WHEELS LIKE THAT, HUH?
PROBABLY ROLLED SOME *HOPHEAD* FOR THE CABBAGE.
PLEASE!
KRESH
KRESH
VROOOM
WHRUNCH
SKREEEECH
POK
PSSSHH

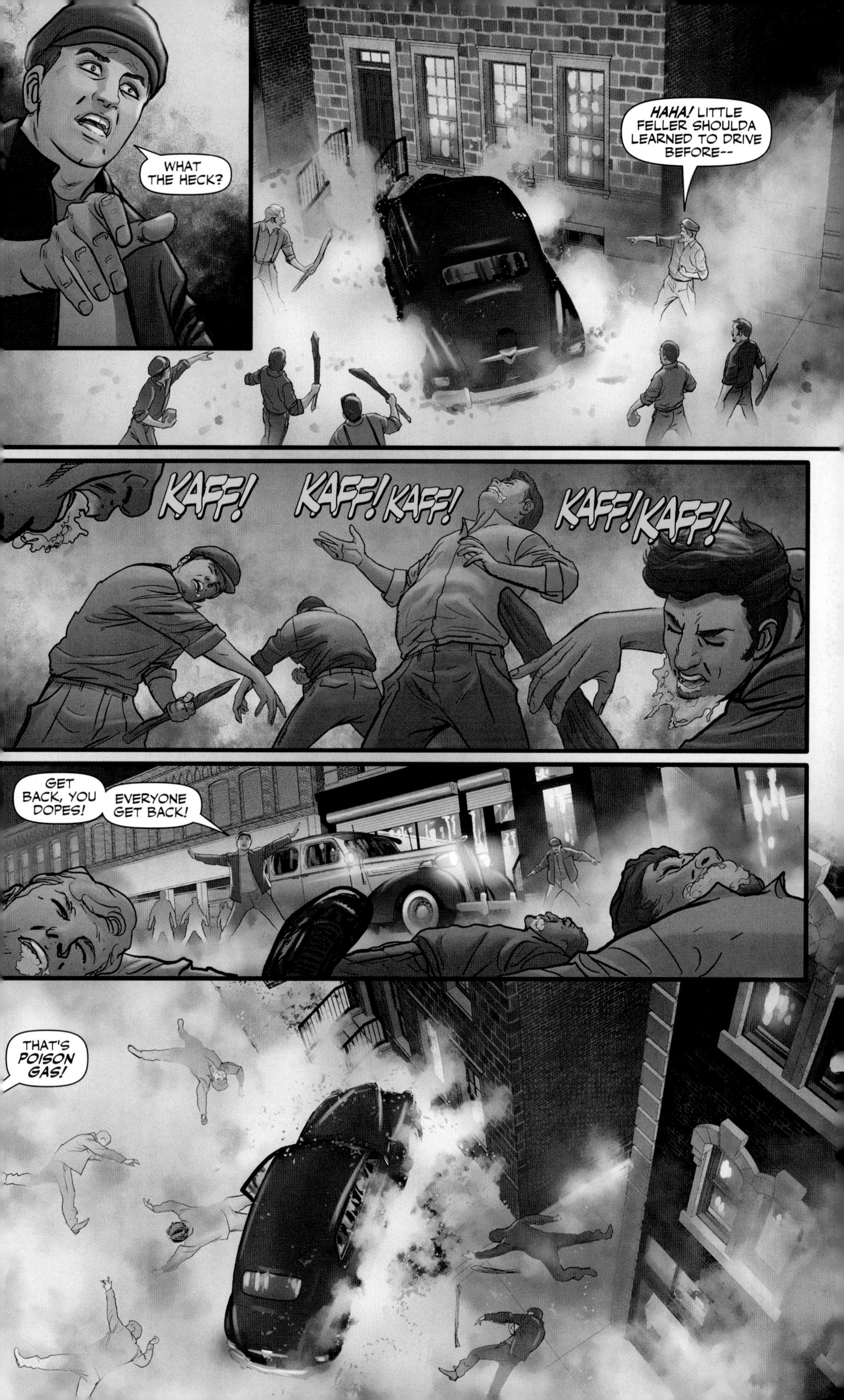
WHAT THE HECK?
HAHA! LITTLE FELLER SHOULDA LEARNED TO DRIVE BEFORE--
KAFF! KAFF! KAFF! KAFF! KAFF!
GET BACK, YOU DOPES!
EVERYONE GET BACK!
THAT'S POISON GAS!

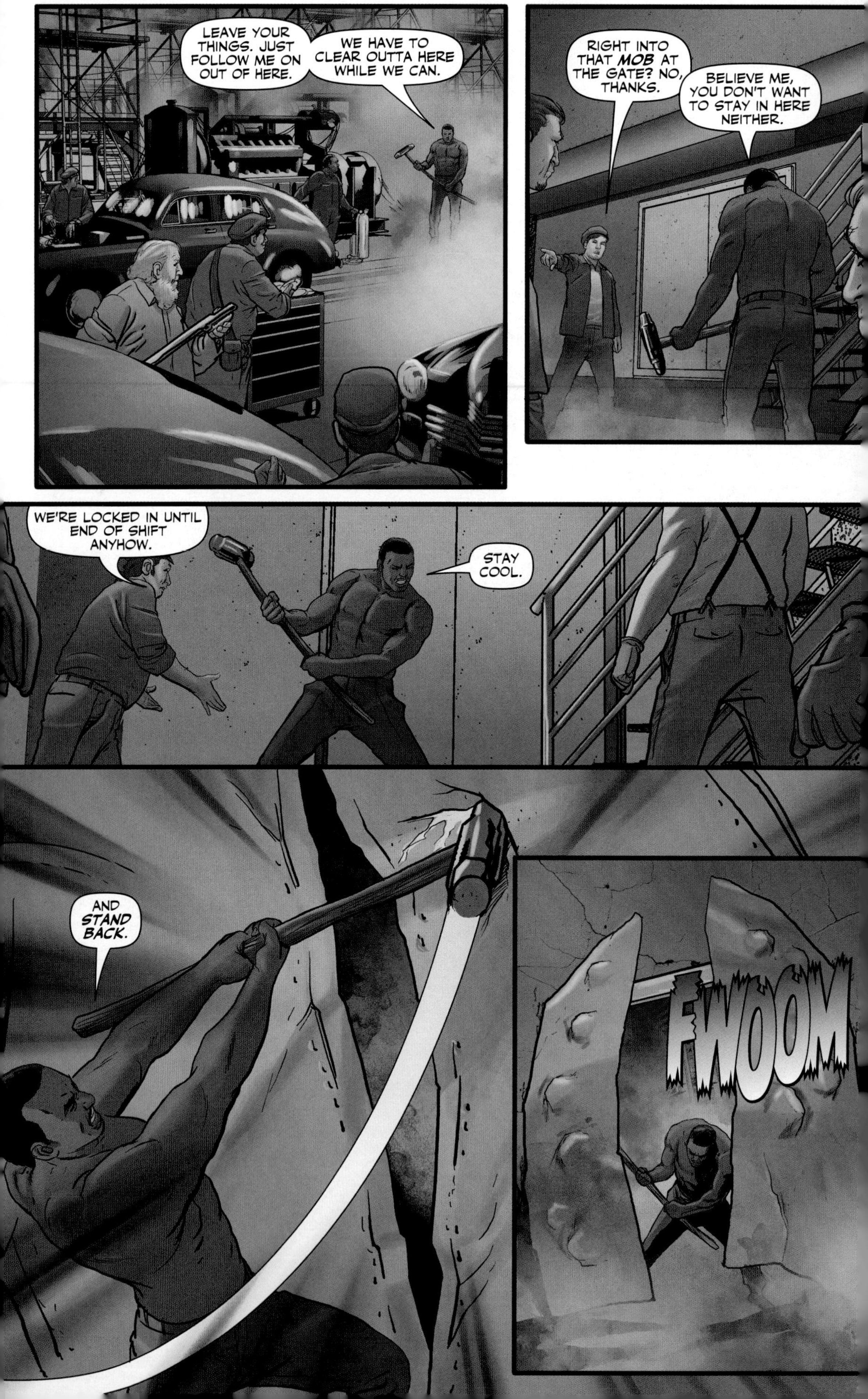
LEAVE YOUR THINGS. JUST FOLLOW ME ON OUT OF HERE.
WE HAVE TO CLEAR OUTTA HERE WHILE WE CAN.
RIGHT INTO THAT MOB AT THE GATE? NO, THANKS.
BELIEVE ME, YOU DON'T WANT TO STAY IN HERE NEITHER.
WE'RE LOCKED IN UNTIL END OF SHIFT ANYHOW.
STAY COOL.
AND STAND BACK.
FWOOM

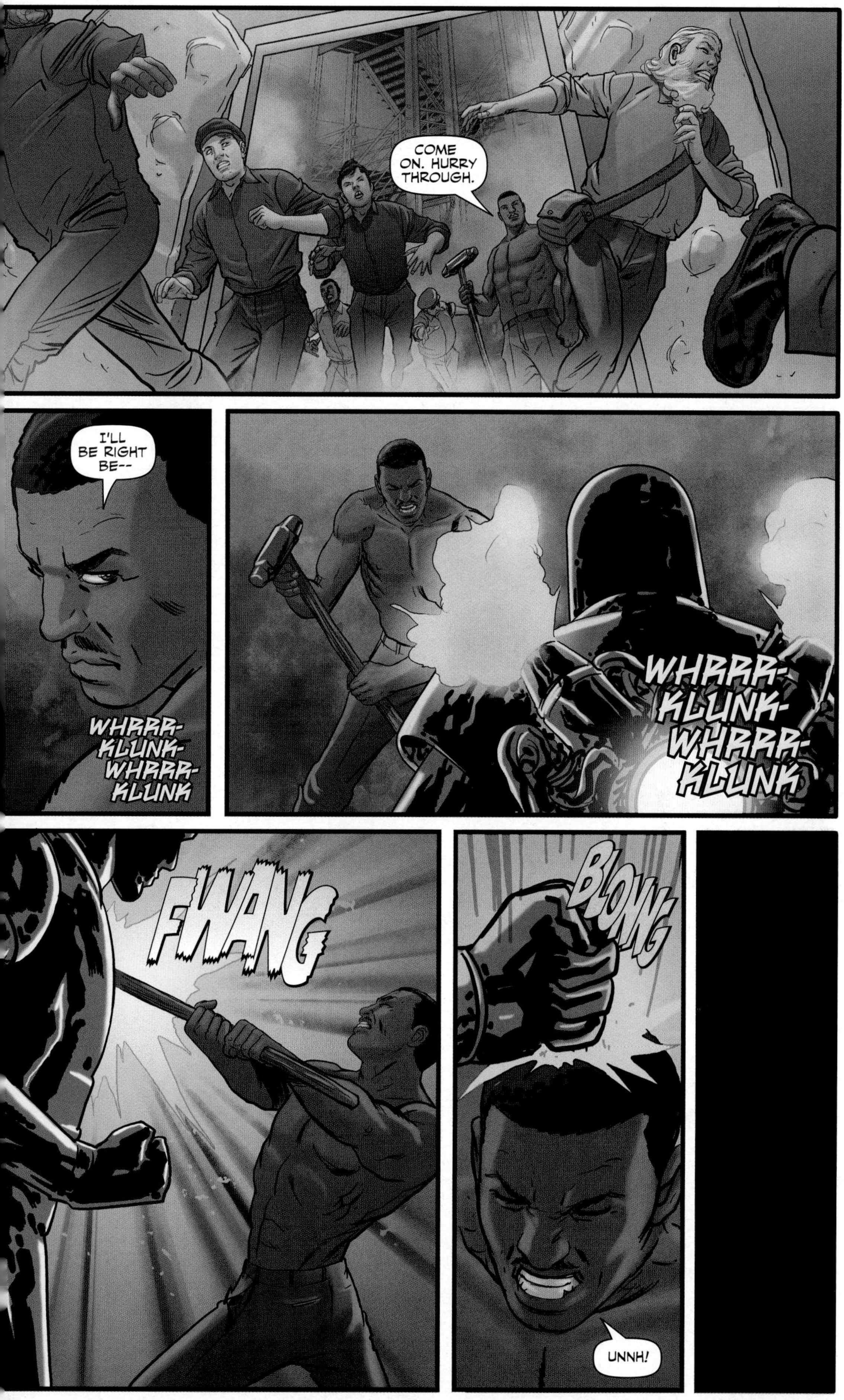
COME ON. HURRY THROUGH.
I'LL BE RIGHT BE--
WHRRR-KLUNK-WHRRR-KLUNK
WHRRR-KLUNK-WHRRR-KLUNK
FWANG
BLONG
UNNH!

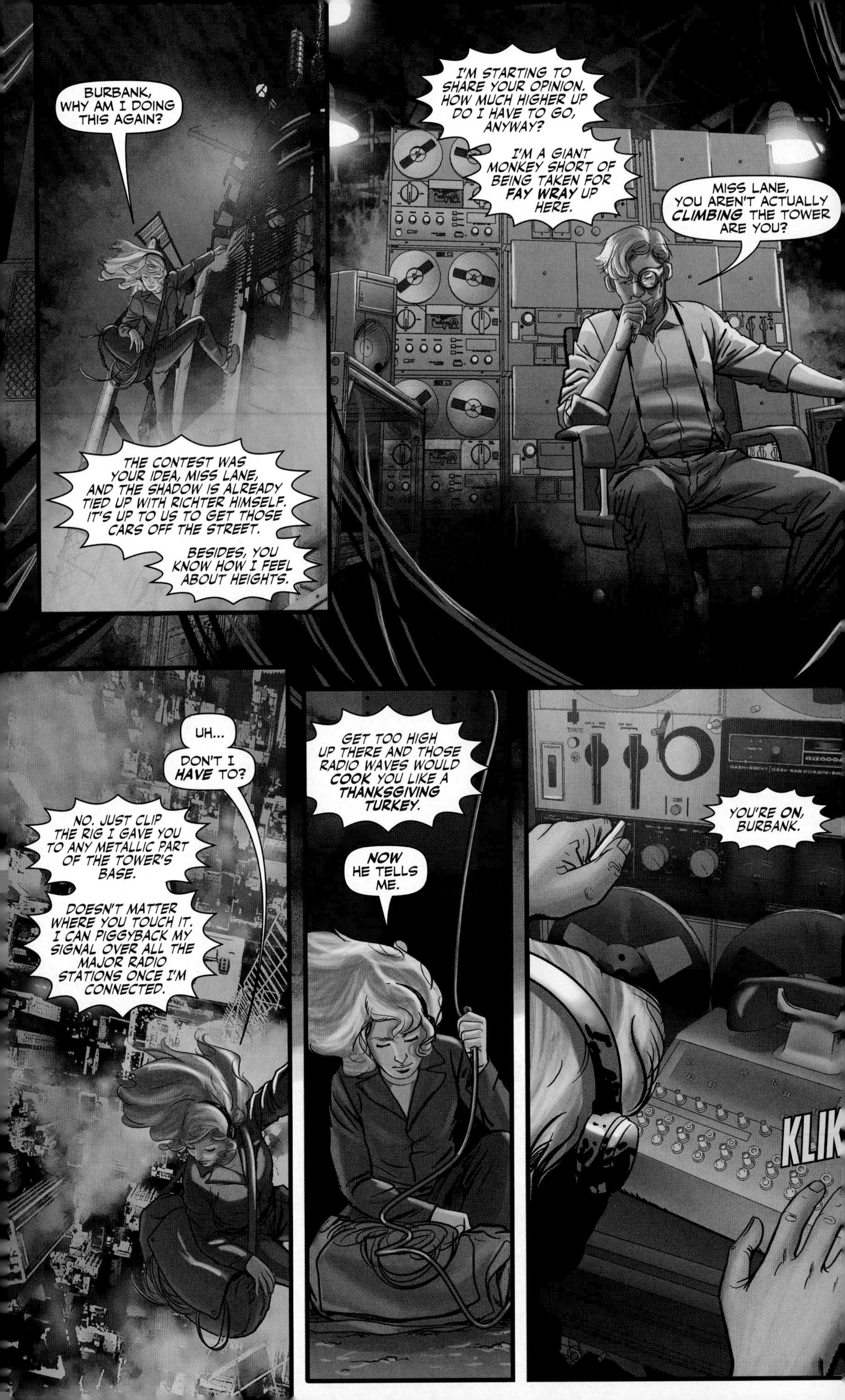
BURBANK, WHY AM I DOING THIS AGAIN?
THE CONTEST WAS YOUR IDEA, MISS LANE, AND THE SHADOW IS ALREADY TIED UP WITH RICHTER HIMSELF. IT'S UP TO US TO GET THOSE CARS OFF THE STREET.
BESIDES, YOU KNOW HOW I FEEL ABOUT HEIGHTS.
I'M STARTING TO SHARE YOUR OPINION. HOW MUCH HIGHER UP DO I HAVE TO GO, ANYWAY?
I'M A GIANT MONKEY SHORT OF BEING TAKEN FOR FAY WRAY UP HERE.
MISS LANE, YOU AREN'T ACTUALLY CLIMBING THE TOWER ARE YOU?
UH...
DON'T I HAVE TO?
NO. JUST CLIP THE RIG I GAVE YOU TO ANY METALLIC PART OF THE TOWER'S BASE.
DOESN'T MATTER WHERE YOU TOUCH IT. I CAN PIGGYBACK MY SIGNAL OVER ALL THE MAJOR RADIO STATIONS ONCE I'M CONNECTED.
GET TOO HIGH UP THERE AND THOSE RADIO WAVES WOULD COOK YOU LIKE A THANKSGIVING TURKEY.
NOW HE TELLS ME.
YOU'RE ON, BURBANK.
KLIK

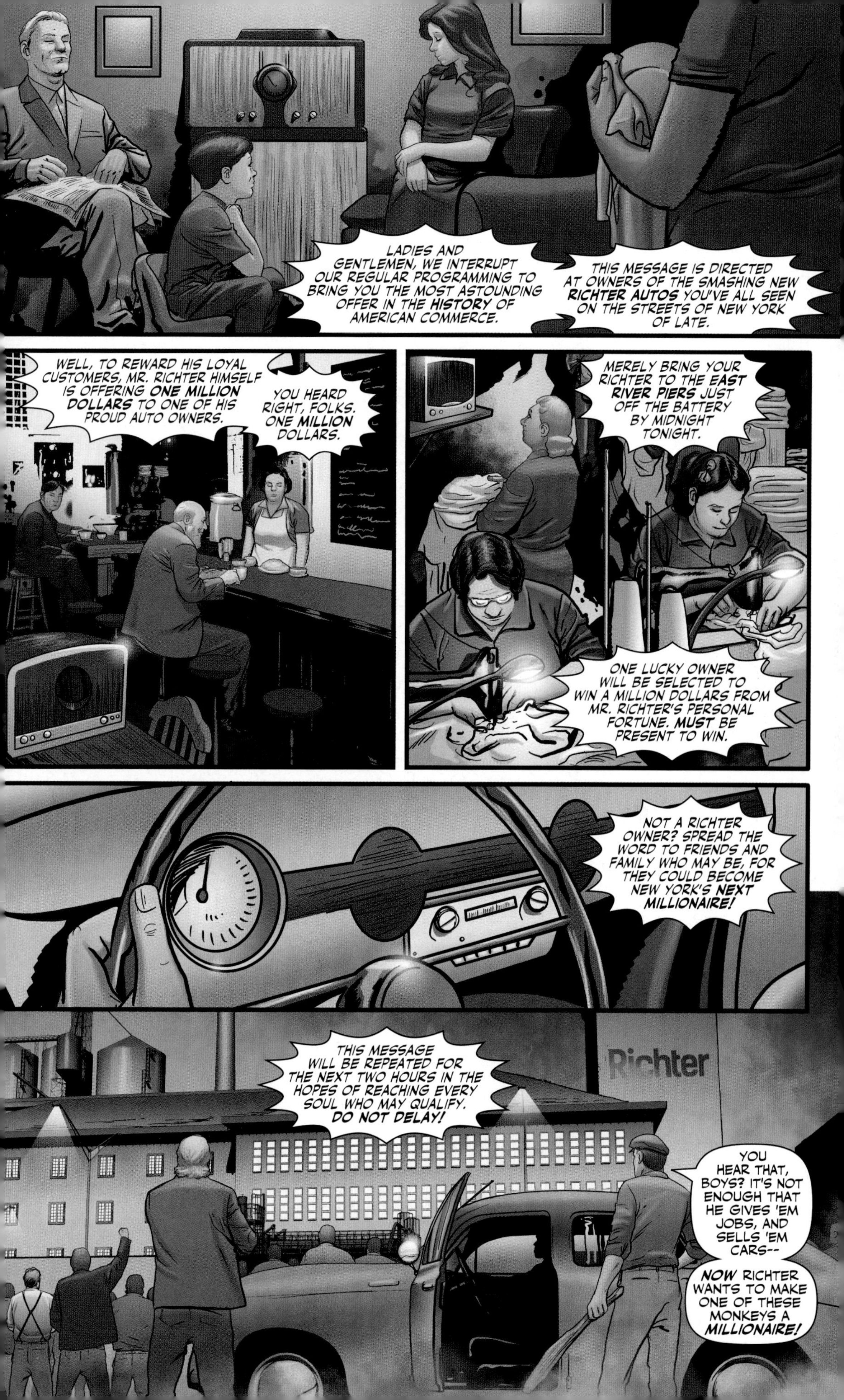
LADIES AND GENTLEMEN, WE INTERRUPT OUR REGULAR PROGRAMMING TO BRING YOU THE MOST ASTOUNDING OFFER IN THE **HISTORY** OF AMERICAN COMMERCE.
THIS MESSAGE IS DIRECTED AT OWNERS OF THE SMASHING NEW **RICHTER AUTOS** YOU'VE ALL SEEN ON THE STREETS OF NEW YORK OF LATE.
WELL, TO REWARD HIS LOYAL CUSTOMERS, MR. RICHTER HIMSELF IS OFFERING **ONE MILLION DOLLARS** TO ONE OF HIS PROUD AUTO OWNERS.
YOU HEARD RIGHT, FOLKS. ONE **MILLION** DOLLARS.
MERELY BRING YOUR RICHTER TO THE **EAST RIVER PIERS** JUST OFF THE BATTERY BY MIDNIGHT TONIGHT.
ONE LUCKY OWNER WILL BE SELECTED TO WIN A MILLION DOLLARS FROM MR. RICHTER'S PERSONAL FORTUNE. **MUST** BE PRESENT TO WIN.
NOT A RICHTER OWNER? SPREAD THE WORD TO FRIENDS AND FAMILY WHO MAY BE, FOR THEY COULD BECOME NEW YORK'S **NEXT MILLIONAIRE!**
THIS MESSAGE WILL BE REPEATED FOR THE NEXT TWO HOURS IN THE HOPES OF REACHING EVERY SOUL WHO MAY QUALIFY. **DO NOT DELAY!**
Richter
YOU HEAR THAT, BOYS? IT'S NOT ENOUGH THAT HE GIVES 'EM JOBS, AND SELLS 'EM CARS--
NOW RICHTER WANTS TO MAKE ONE OF THESE MONKEYS A **MILLIONAIRE!**

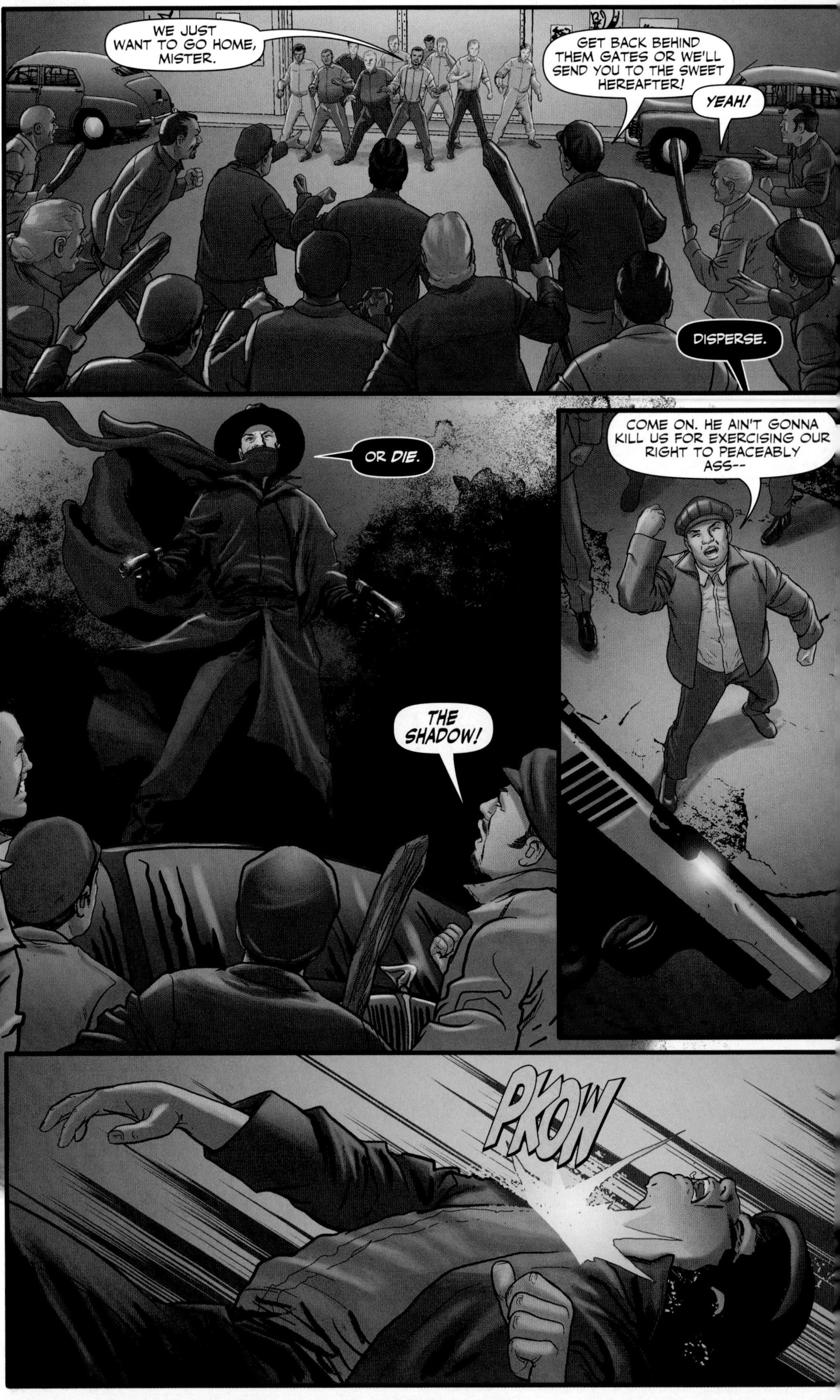
WE JUST WANT TO GO HOME, MISTER.
GET BACK BEHIND THEM GATES OR WE'LL SEND YOU TO THE SWEET HEREAFTER!
YEAH!
DISPERSE.
OR DIE.
THE SHADOW!
COME ON. HE AIN'T GONNA KILL US FOR EXERCISING OUR RIGHT TO PEACEABLY ASS--
PKOW

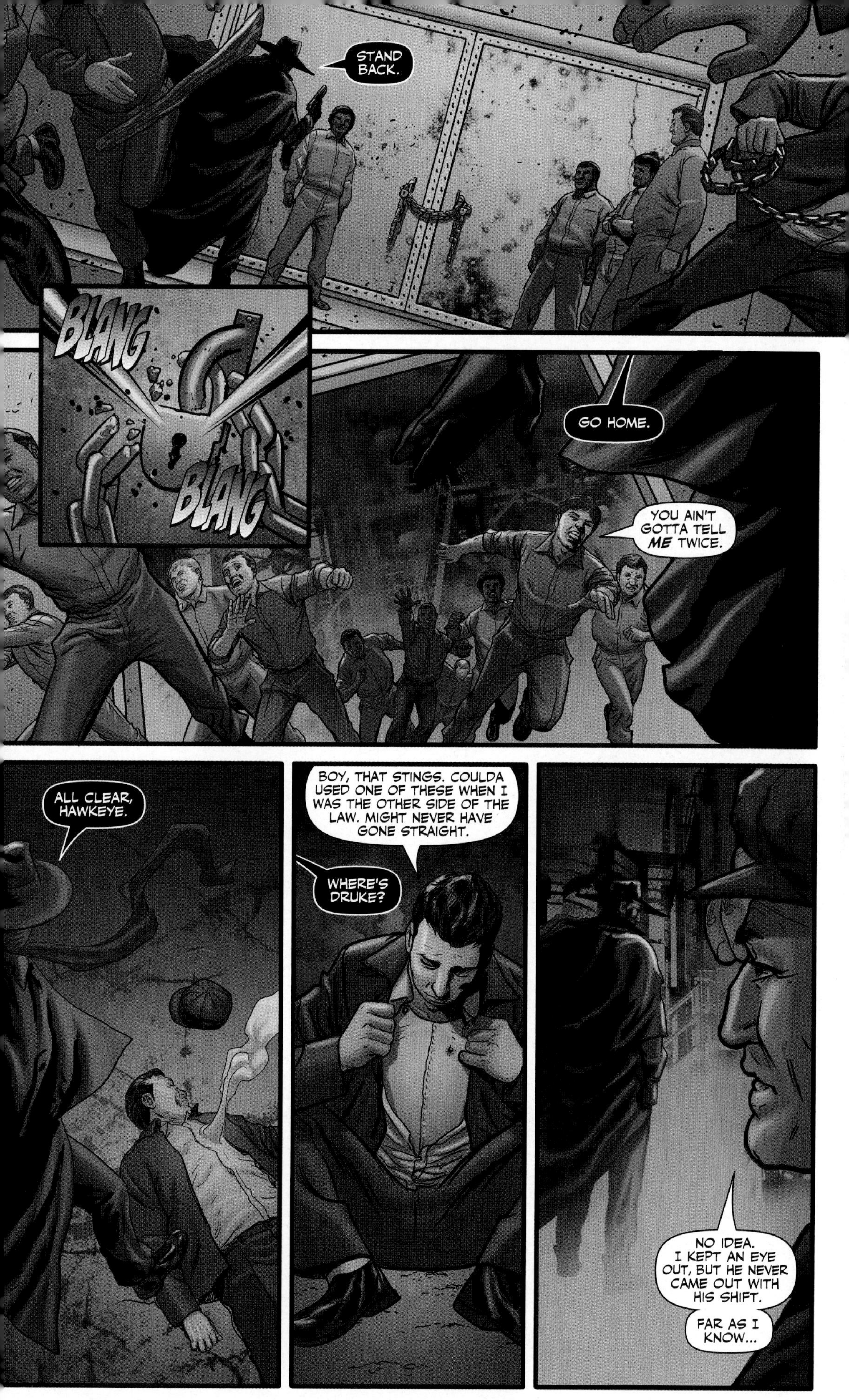
STAND BACK.
BLANG
BLANG
GO HOME.
YOU AIN'T GOTTA TELL **ME** TWICE.
ALL CLEAR, HAWKEYE.
BOY, THAT STINGS. COULDA USED ONE OF THESE WHEN I WAS THE OTHER SIDE OF THE LAW. MIGHT NEVER HAVE GONE STRAIGHT.
WHERE'S DRUKE?
NO IDEA. I KEPT AN EYE OUT, BUT HE NEVER CAME OUT WITH HIS SHIFT.
FAR AS I KNOW...

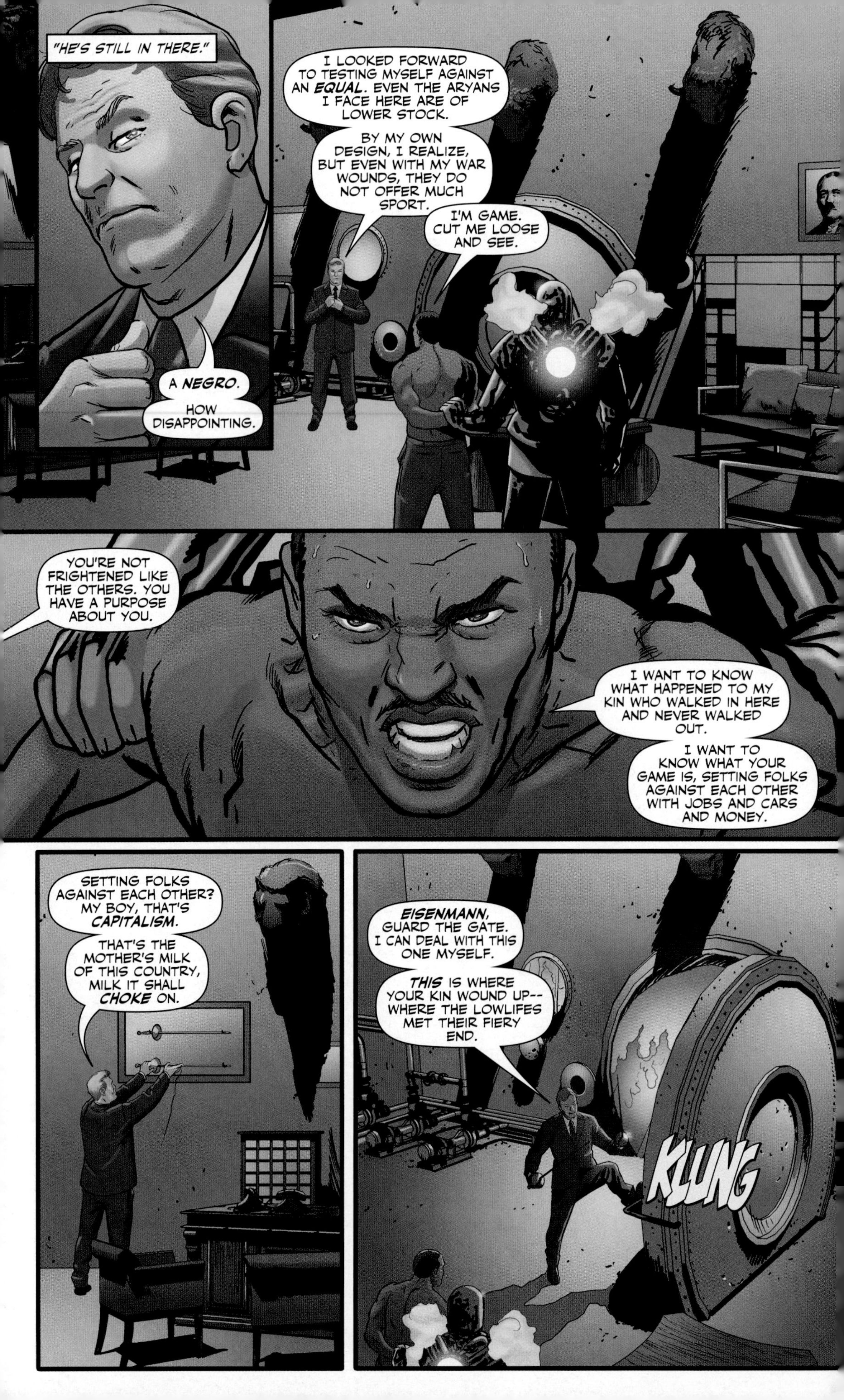
"HE'S STILL IN THERE."
A NEGRO.
HOW DISAPPOINTING.
I LOOKED FORWARD TO TESTING MYSELF AGAINST AN EQUAL. EVEN THE ARYANS I FACE HERE ARE OF LOWER STOCK.
BY MY OWN DESIGN, I REALIZE, BUT EVEN WITH MY WAR WOUNDS, THEY DO NOT OFFER MUCH SPORT.
I'M GAME. CUT ME LOOSE AND SEE.
YOU'RE NOT FRIGHTENED LIKE THE OTHERS. YOU HAVE A PURPOSE ABOUT YOU.
I WANT TO KNOW WHAT HAPPENED TO MY KIN WHO WALKED IN HERE AND NEVER WALKED OUT.
I WANT TO KNOW WHAT YOUR GAME IS, SETTING FOLKS AGAINST EACH OTHER WITH JOBS AND CARS AND MONEY.
SETTING FOLKS AGAINST EACH OTHER? MY BOY, THAT'S CAPITALISM.
THAT'S THE MOTHER'S MILK OF THIS COUNTRY, MILK IT SHALL CHOKE ON.
EISENMANN, GUARD THE GATE. I CAN DEAL WITH THIS ONE MYSELF.
THIS IS WHERE YOUR KIN WOUND UP-- WHERE THE LOWLIFES MET THEIR FIERY END.
KLUNG

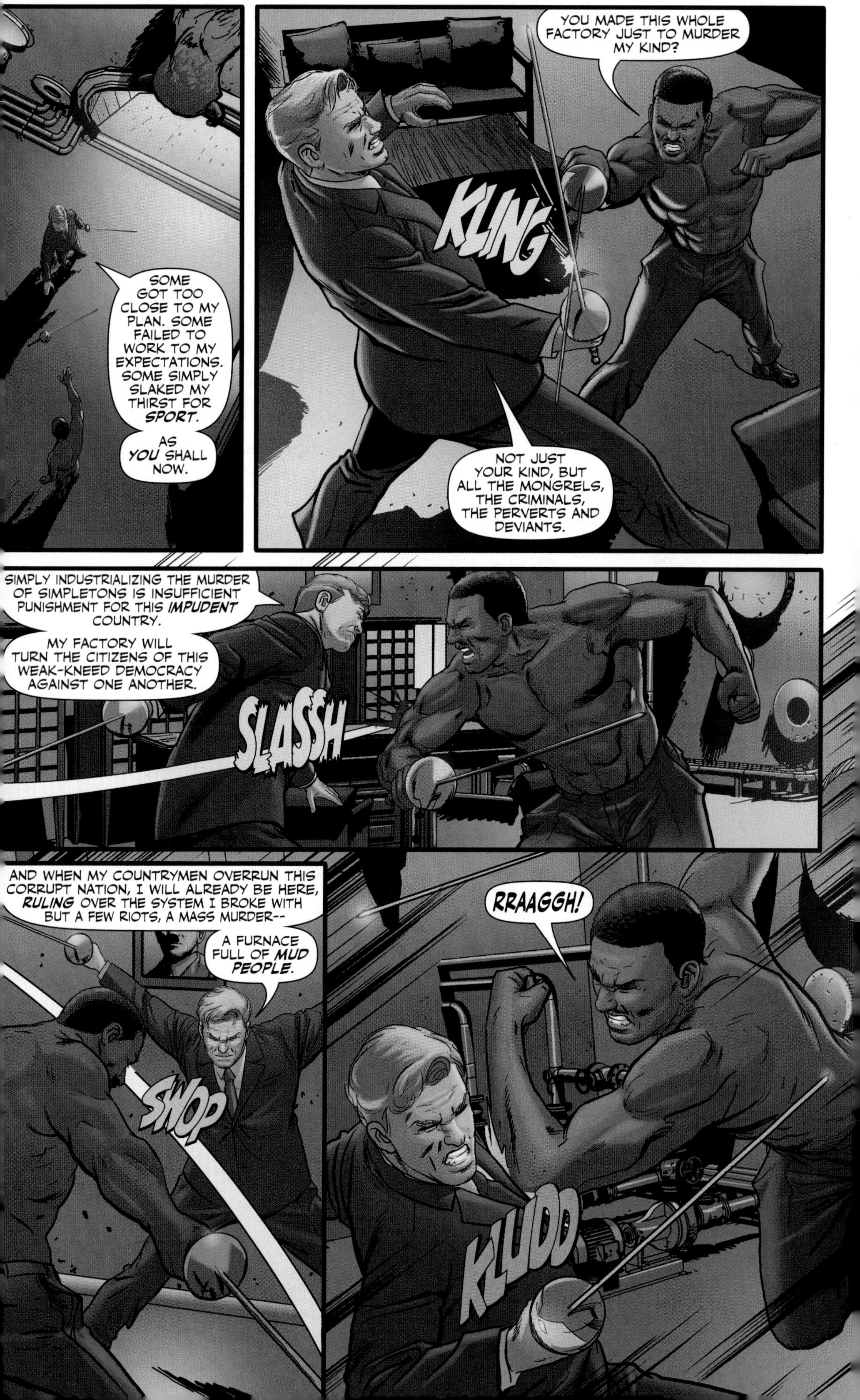
SOME GOT TOO CLOSE TO MY PLAN. SOME FAILED TO WORK TO MY EXPECTATIONS. SOME SIMPLY SLAKED MY THIRST FOR SPORT.
AS YOU SHALL NOW.
YOU MADE THIS WHOLE FACTORY JUST TO MURDER MY KIND?
KLING
NOT JUST YOUR KIND, BUT ALL THE MONGRELS, THE CRIMINALS, THE PERVERTS AND DEVIANTS.
SIMPLY INDUSTRIALIZING THE MURDER OF SIMPLETONS IS INSUFFICIENT PUNISHMENT FOR THIS IMPUDENT COUNTRY.
MY FACTORY WILL TURN THE CITIZENS OF THIS WEAK-KNEED DEMOCRACY AGAINST ONE ANOTHER.
SLASSH
AND WHEN MY COUNTRYMEN OVERRUN THIS CORRUPT NATION, I WILL ALREADY BE HERE, RULING OVER THE SYSTEM I BROKE WITH BUT A FEW RIOTS, A MASS MURDER--
A FURNACE FULL OF MUD PEOPLE.
SWOP
RRAAGGH!
KLUDD

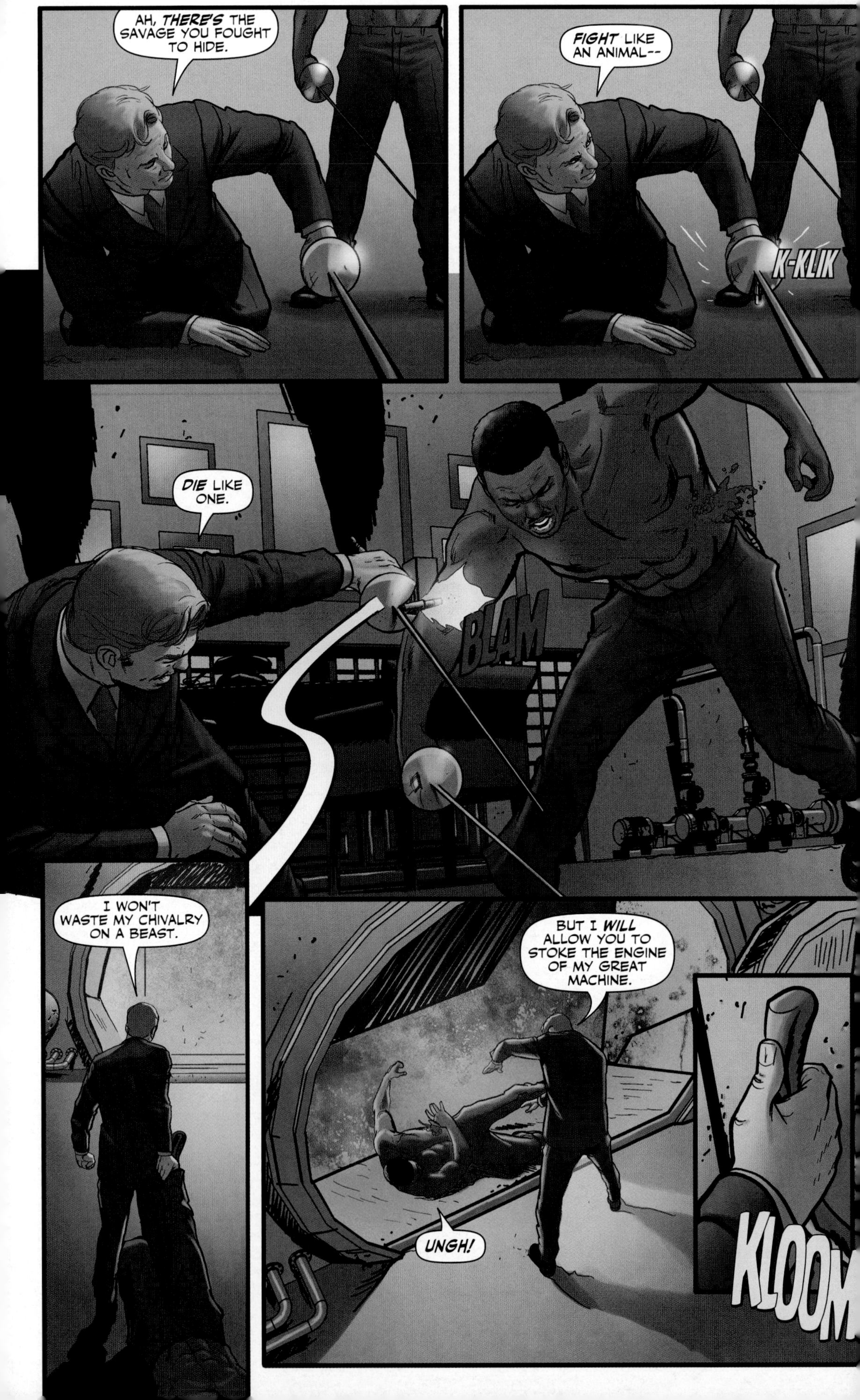
AH, *THERE'S* THE SAVAGE YOU FOUGHT TO HIDE.
FIGHT LIKE AN ANIMAL--
K-KLIK
DIE LIKE ONE.
BLAM
I WON'T WASTE MY CHIVALRY ON A BEAST.
BUT I *WILL* ALLOW YOU TO STOKE THE ENGINE OF MY GREAT MACHINE.
UNGH!
KLOOM

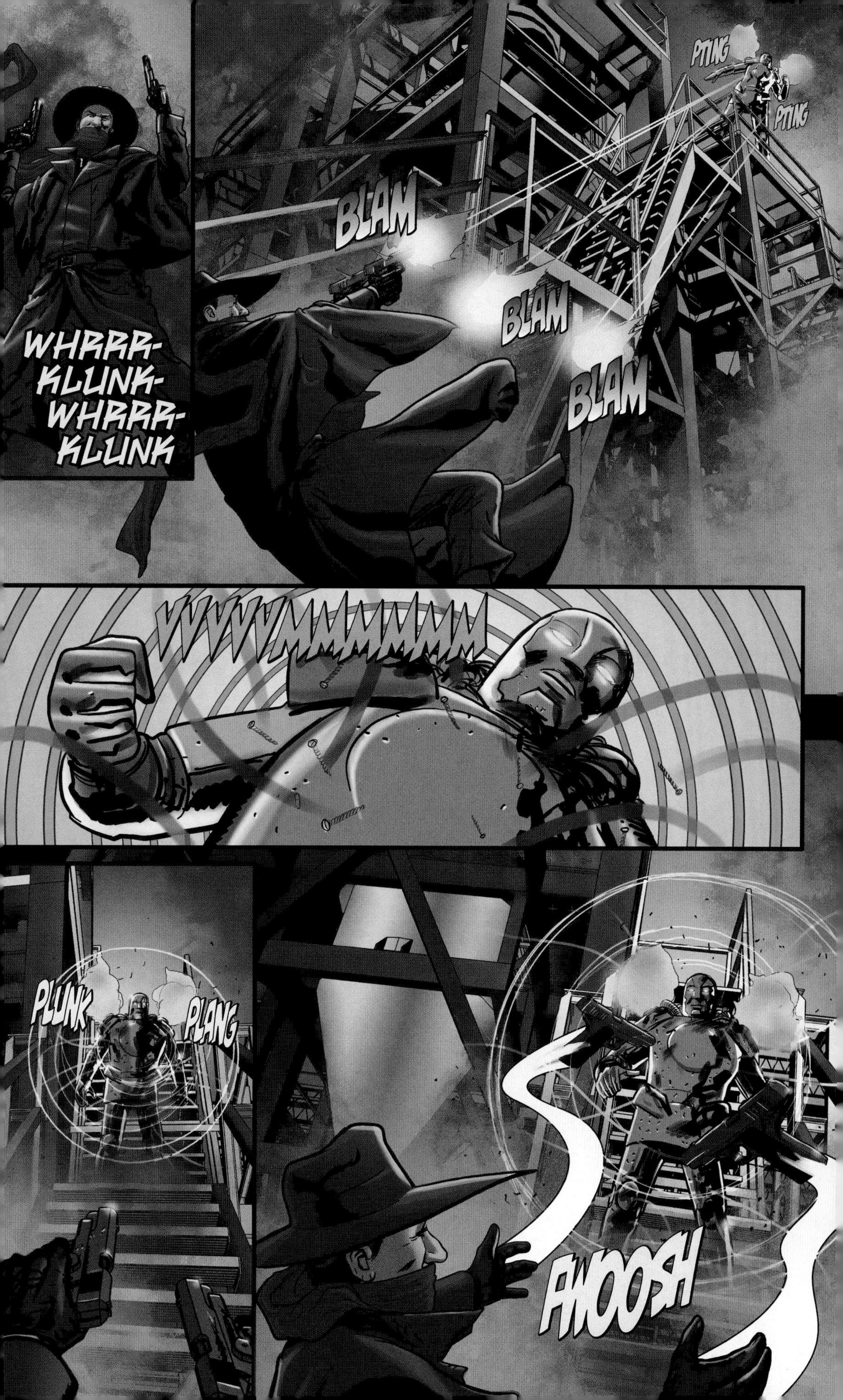
WHRRR-
KLUNK-
WHRRR-
KLUNK
PTING
PTING
BLAM
BLAM
BLAM
VVVVMMMMMMM
PLUNK
PLANG
FWOOSH

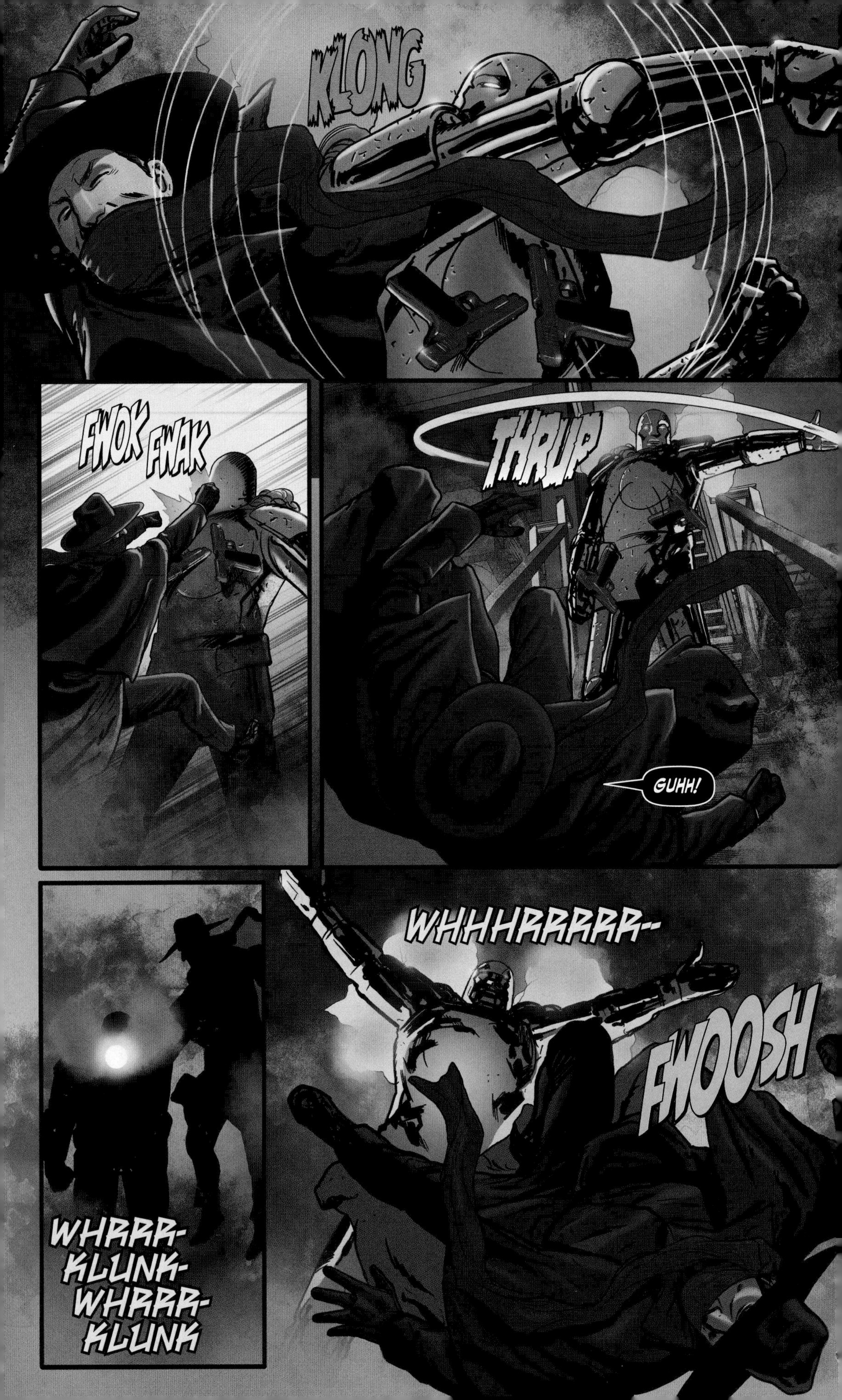
KLONG
FWOK FWAK
THRUP
GUHH!
WHRRR-
KLUNK-
WHRRR-
KLUNK
WHHHRRRRR-
FWOOSH

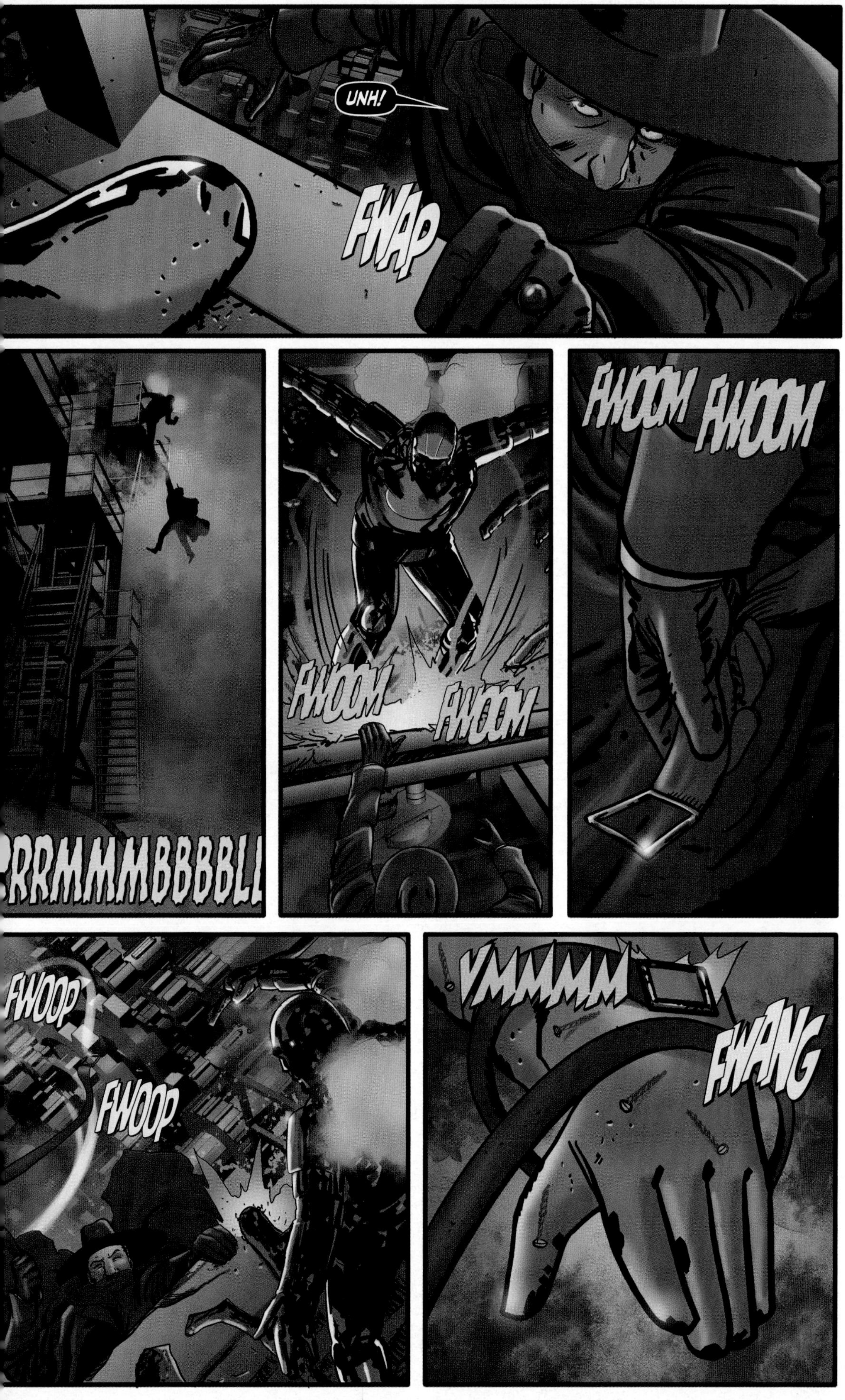
UNH!
FWAP
RRMMMMBBBBLL
FWOOM
FWOOM
FWOOM FWOOM
FWOOP
FWOOP
VMMMM
FWANG

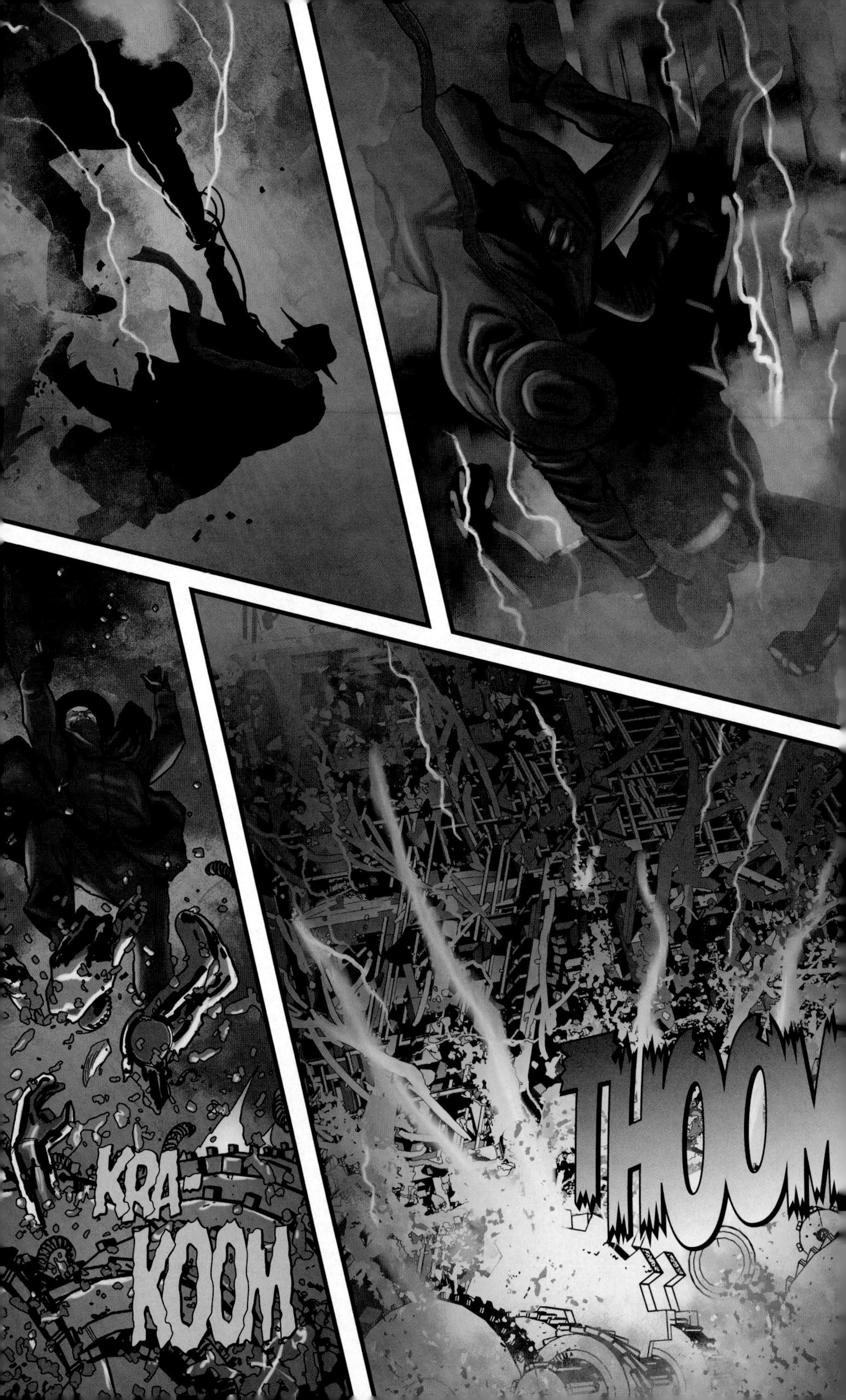
KRA-
KOOM
THOOM

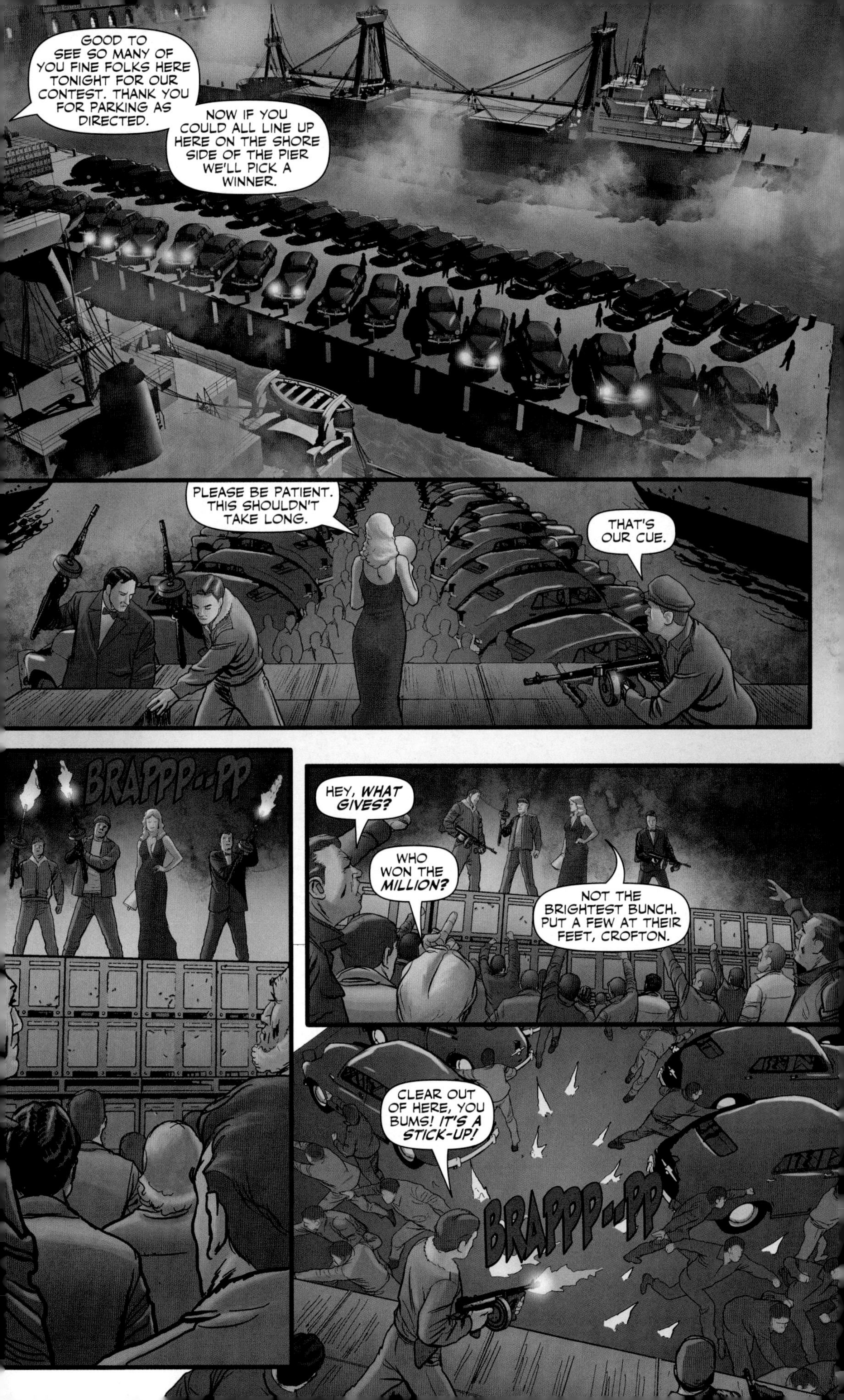
GOOD TO SEE SO MANY OF YOU FINE FOLKS HERE TONIGHT FOR OUR CONTEST. THANK YOU FOR PARKING AS DIRECTED.
NOW IF YOU COULD ALL LINE UP HERE ON THE SHORE SIDE OF THE PIER WE'LL PICK A WINNER.
PLEASE BE PATIENT. THIS SHOULDN'T TAKE LONG.
THAT'S OUR CUE.
BRAPPP--PP
HEY, *WHAT GIVES?*
WHO WON THE *MILLION?*
NOT THE BRIGHTEST BUNCH. PUT A FEW AT THEIR FEET, CROFTON.
CLEAR OUT OF HERE, YOU BUMS! *IT'S A STICK-UP!*
BRAPPP--PP

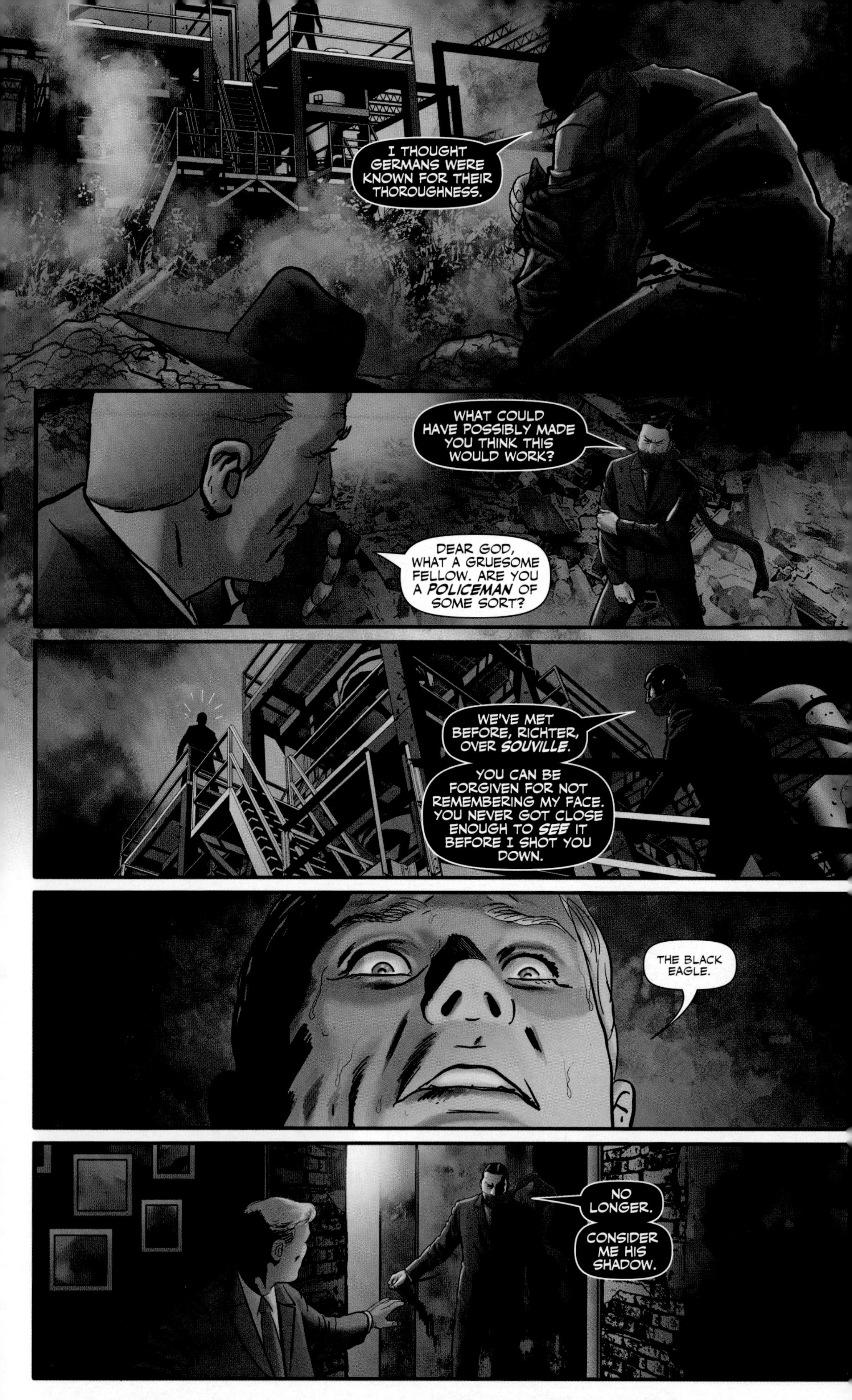
I THOUGHT GERMANS WERE KNOWN FOR THEIR THOROUGHNESS.
WHAT COULD HAVE POSSIBLY MADE YOU THINK THIS WOULD WORK?
DEAR GOD, WHAT A GRUESOME FELLOW. ARE YOU A POLICEMAN OF SOME SORT?
WE'VE MET BEFORE, RICHTER, OVER SOUVILLE.
YOU CAN BE FORGIVEN FOR NOT REMEMBERING MY FACE. YOU NEVER GOT CLOSE ENOUGH TO SEE IT BEFORE I SHOT YOU DOWN.
THE BLACK EAGLE.
NO LONGER.
CONSIDER ME HIS SHADOW.

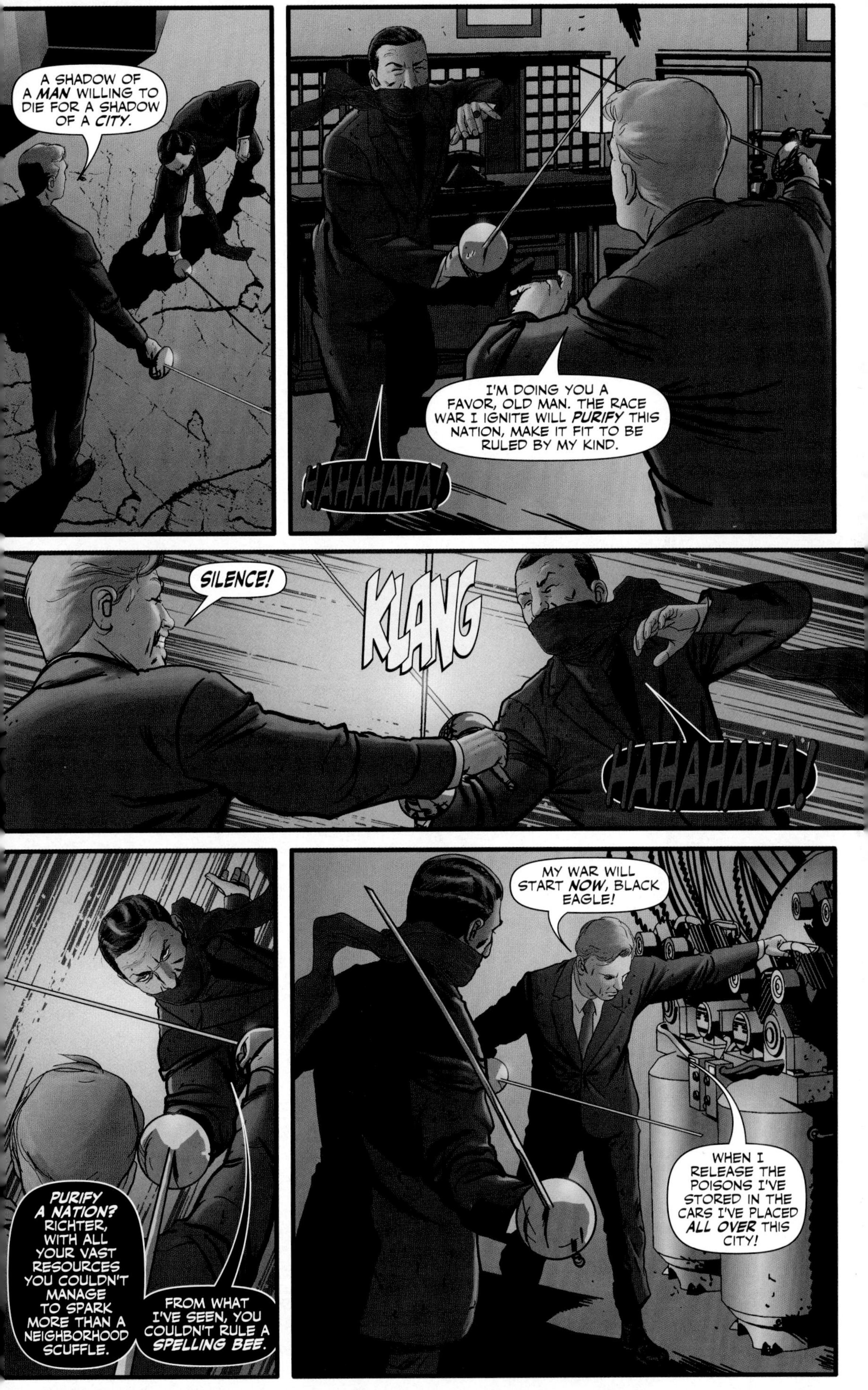
A SHADOW OF A *MAN* WILLING TO DIE FOR A SHADOW OF A *CITY*.
I'M DOING YOU A FAVOR, OLD MAN. THE RACE WAR I IGNITE WILL *PURIFY* THIS NATION, MAKE IT FIT TO BE RULED BY MY KIND.
HAHAHAHA!
SILENCE!
KLANG
HAHAHAHA!
PURIFY A NATION? RICHTER, WITH ALL YOUR VAST RESOURCES YOU COULDN'T MANAGE TO SPARK MORE THAN A NEIGHBORHOOD SCUFFLE.
FROM WHAT I'VE SEEN, YOU COULDN'T RULE A *SPELLING BEE*.
MY WAR WILL START *NOW*, BLACK EAGLE!
WHEN I RELEASE THE POISONS I'VE STORED IN THE CARS I'VE PLACED *ALL OVER* THIS CITY!

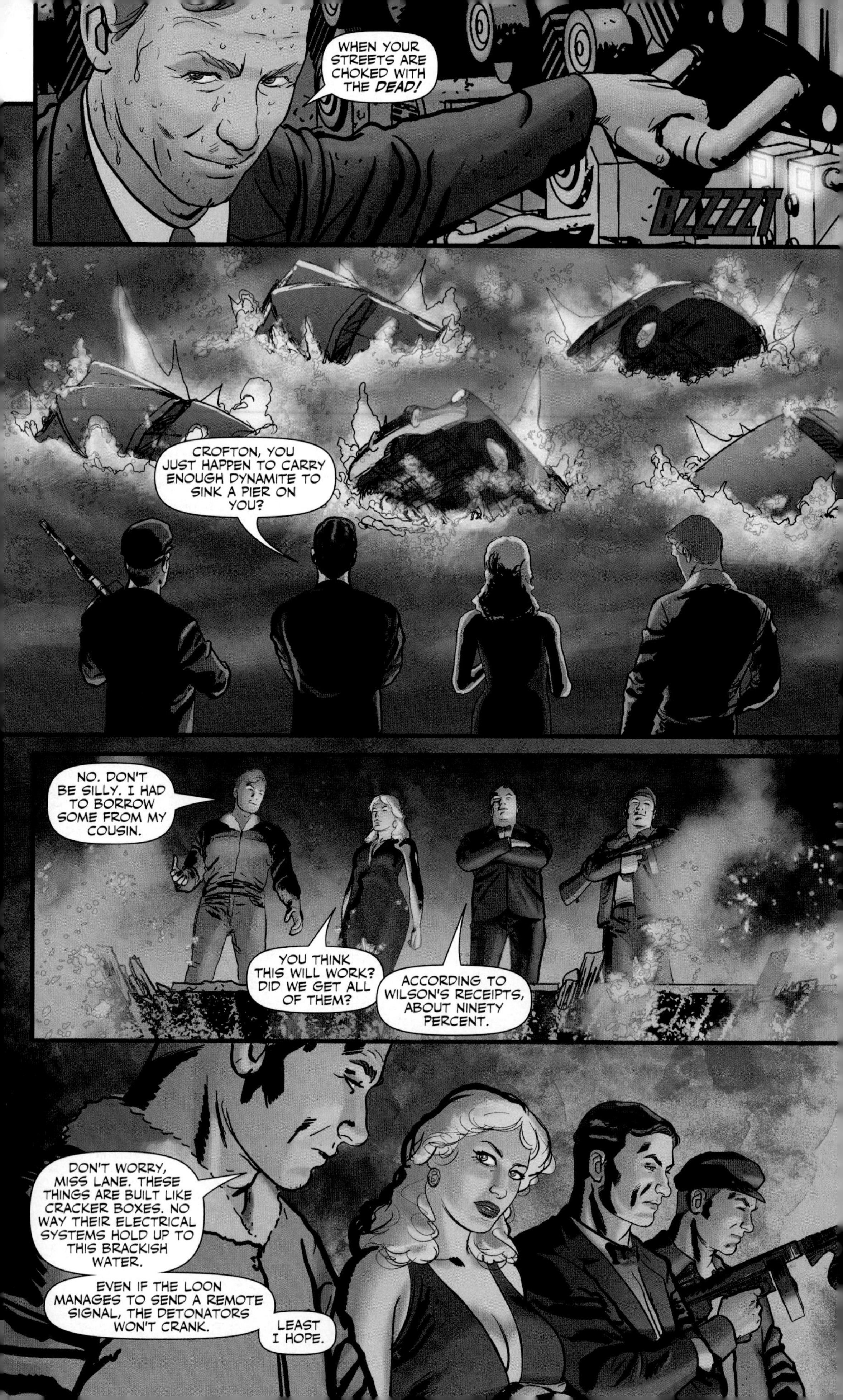
WHEN YOUR STREETS ARE CHOKED WITH THE *DEAD!*
BZZZZZT
CROFTON, YOU JUST HAPPEN TO CARRY ENOUGH DYNAMITE TO SINK A PIER ON YOU?
NO. DON'T BE SILLY. I HAD TO BORROW SOME FROM MY COUSIN.
YOU THINK THIS WILL WORK? DID WE GET ALL OF THEM?
ACCORDING TO WILSON'S RECEIPTS, ABOUT NINETY PERCENT.
DON'T WORRY, MISS LANE. THESE THINGS ARE BUILT LIKE CRACKER BOXES. NO WAY THEIR ELECTRICAL SYSTEMS HOLD UP TO THIS BRACKISH WATER.
EVEN IF THE LOON MANAGES TO SEND A REMOTE SIGNAL, THE DETONATORS WON'T CRANK.
LEAST I HOPE.

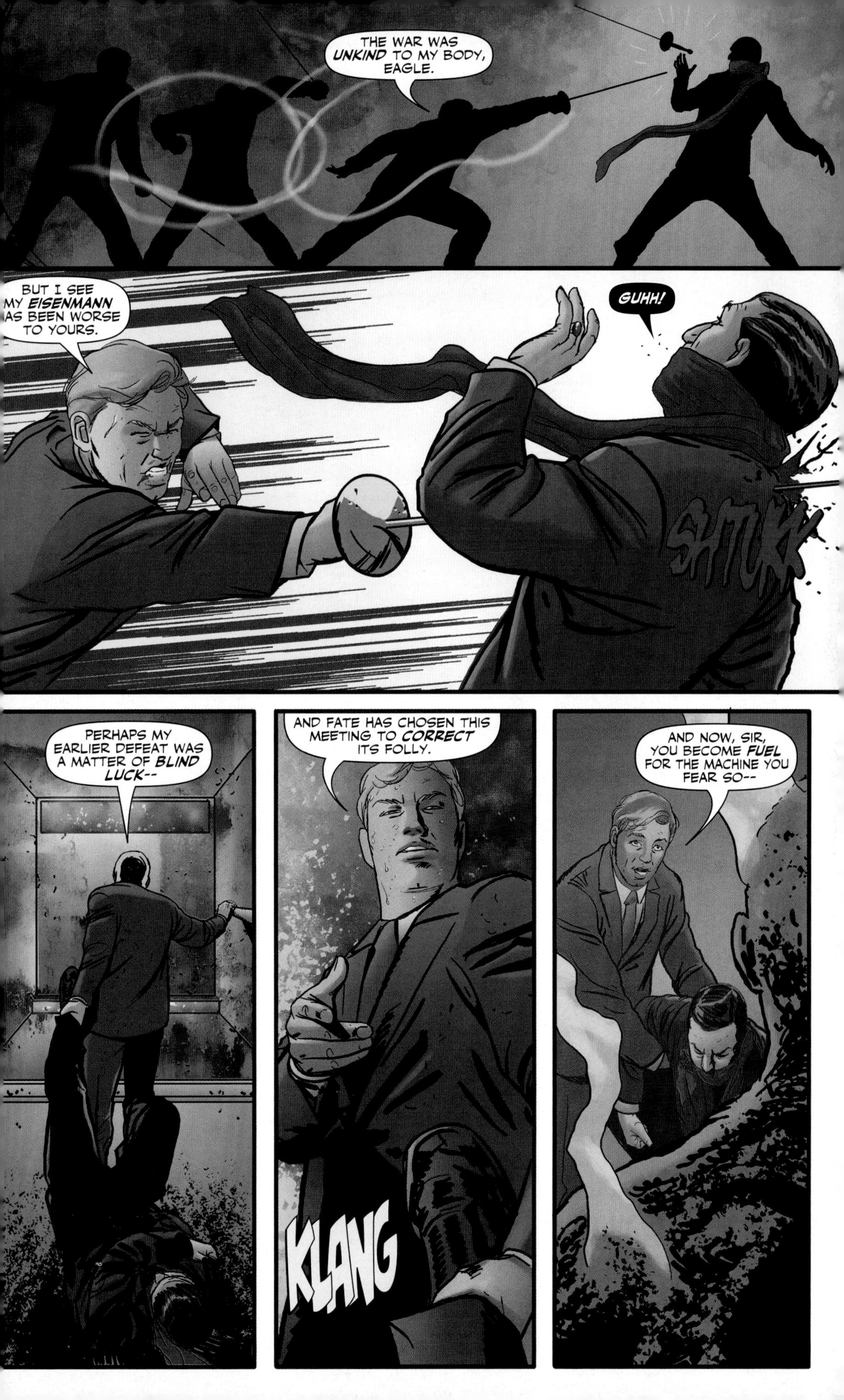
THE WAR WAS UNKIND TO MY BODY, EAGLE.
BUT I SEE MY EISENMANN HAS BEEN WORSE TO YOURS.
GUHH!
SHTUKK
PERHAPS MY EARLIER DEFEAT WAS A MATTER OF BLIND LUCK--
AND FATE HAS CHOSEN THIS MEETING TO CORRECT ITS FOLLY.
KLANG
AND NOW, SIR, YOU BECOME FUEL FOR THE MACHINE YOU FEAR SO--

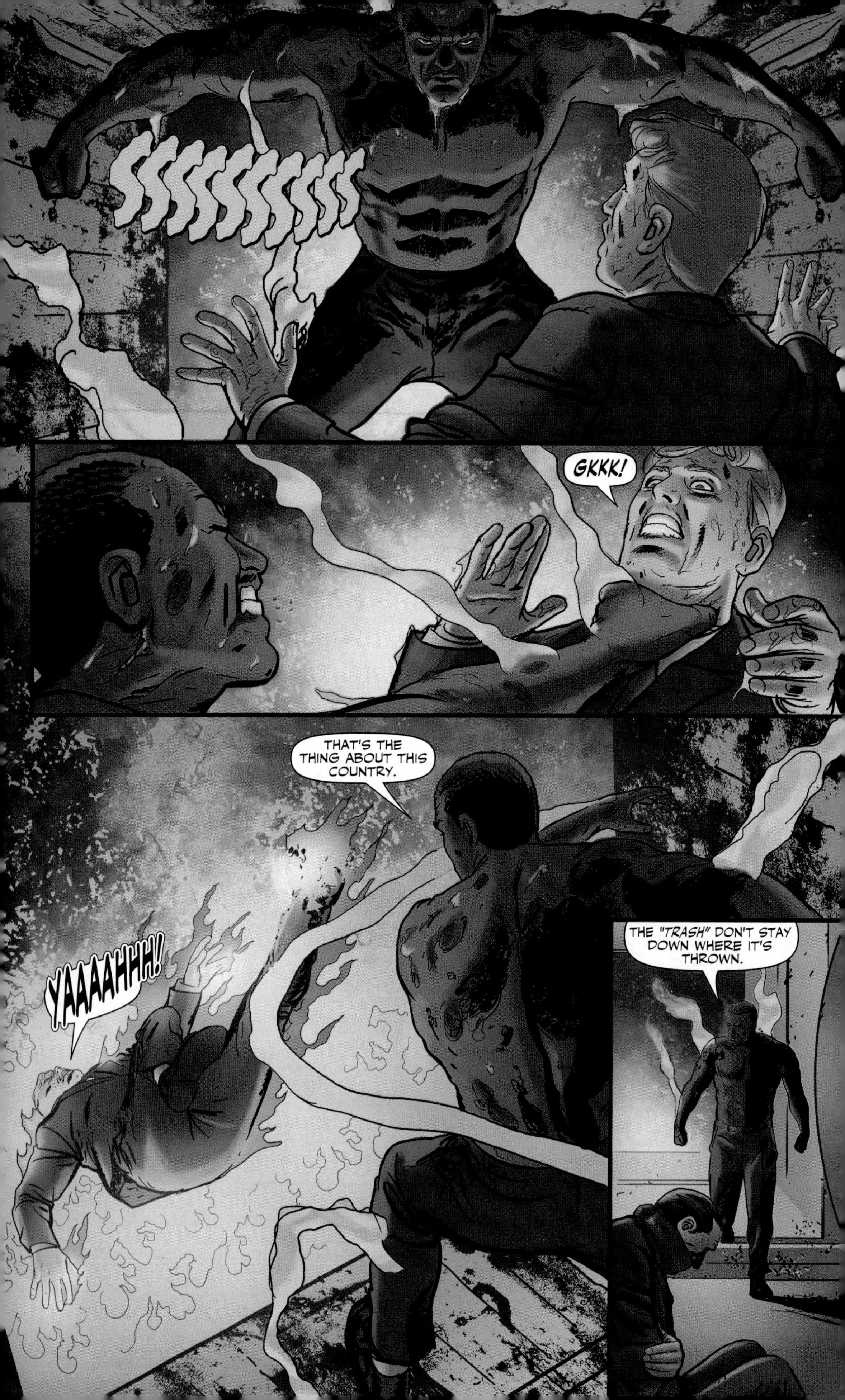
SSSSSSSSSSS
GKKK!
THAT'S THE THING ABOUT THIS COUNTRY.
YAAAAHHH!
THE "TRASH" DON'T STAY DOWN WHERE IT'S THROWN.

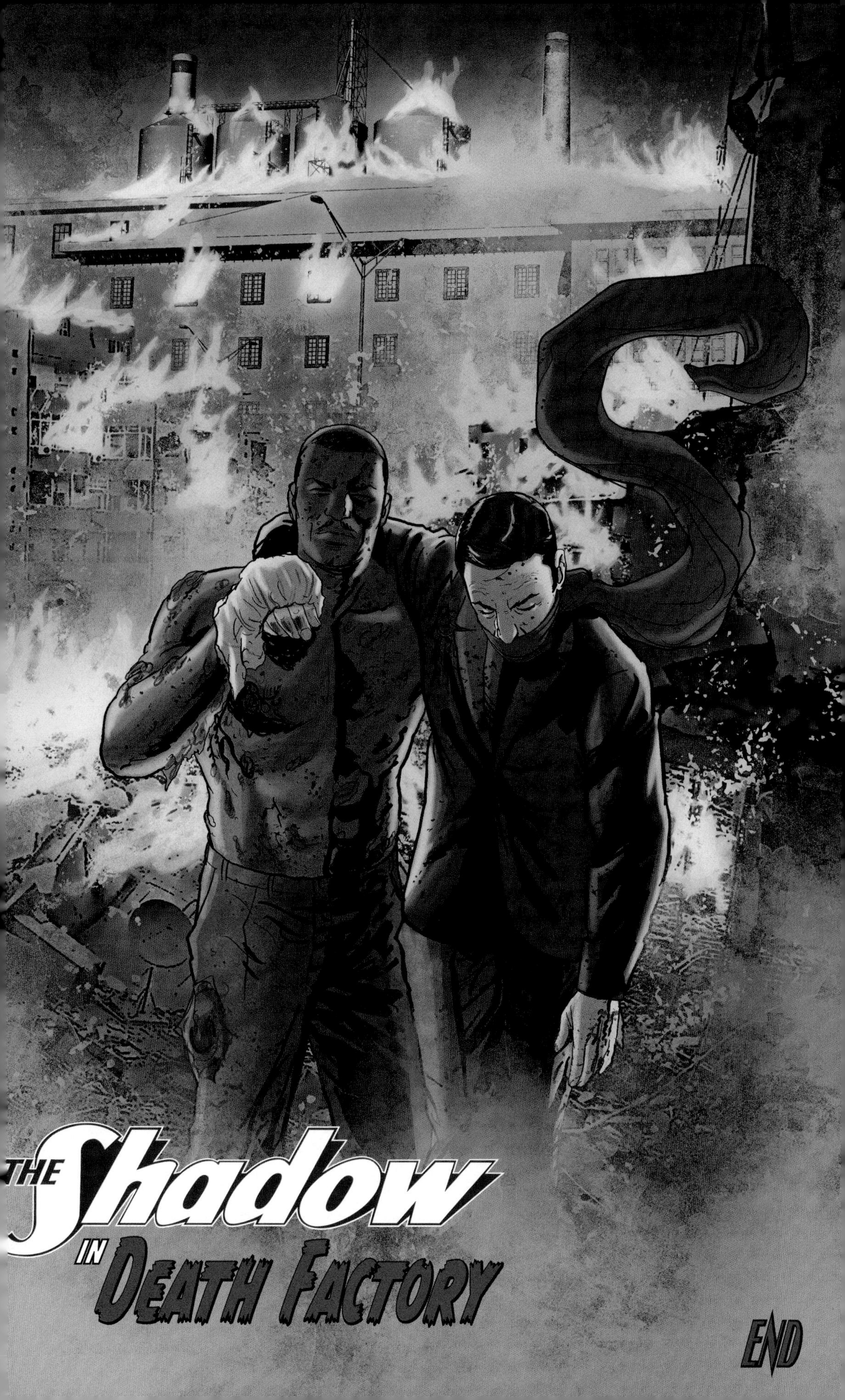
THE Shadow
IN DEATH FACTORY
END

CASTING SHADOWS

A LOOK AT THE MAKING OF *THE SHADOW: DEATH FACTORY* FROM SCRIPT TO FINAL PAGE

script by PHIL HESTER
art by IVAN RODRIGUEZ
colors by IMPACTO STUDIOS
letters by ROB STEEN

PAGE ONE

PANEL ONE:
Circa 1936. This is classic pulpy Shadow prime beef.

> SHADOW CAP: You don't need special powers of perception to know what evil lurks in the hearts of men.

PANEL TWO:
Low angle on The Shadow using a fire escape or gutter pipe or something to control his fa
as he vaults down the side of a dilapidated warehouse.

> SHADOW CAP: It doesn't lurk.

PANEL THREE:
Closer on the Shadow as he carefully noses through a shattered window, his guns drawn.

> SHADOW CAP: It walks across their faces.

> SHADOW CAP: It stands on their shoulders.

> SHADOW CAP: It leaps from their open mouths.

PANEL FOUR:
Wider shot. We can see The Shadow is stalking across a catwalk inside a large warehouse. Its dark and maze-like. Have fun. He's headed for a small wooden door at the end of the cat walk near the top of the wall, like a portal between two sides of the large building which is separated by a brick wall, now shut. (see ref pic attached)

> SHADOW CAP: Men don't hide their evil at all.

> SHADOW CAP: They burnish it to a high shine and set it in their front windows.

> SHADOW CAP: They prune and feed it to keep it in bloom.

PANEL FOUR:
Behind The Shadow as he kicks the rotted wood door open with his heel, shattering it.

> SFX: Kroom!

> SHADOW CAP: They just don't call it evil.

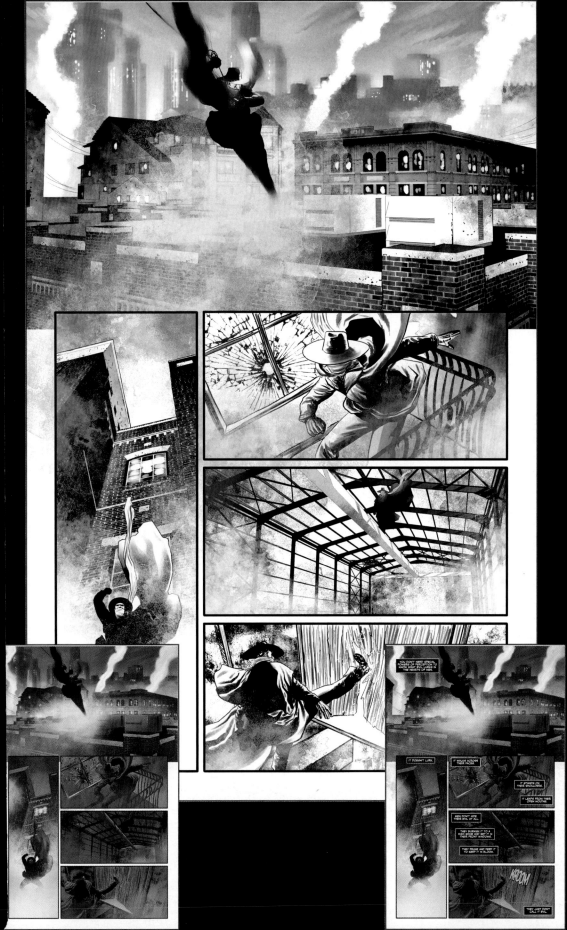

YOU DON'T NEED SPECIAL POWERS OR PERCEPTION TO KNOW WHAT EVIL LURKS IN THE HEARTS OF MEN.

IT DOESN'T LURK.

IT WALKS ACROSS THEIR FACES.

IT STANDS ON THEIR SHOULDERS.

IT LEAPS FROM THEIR OPEN MOUTHS.

MEN DON'T HIDE THEIR EVIL AT ALL.

THEY BURNISH IT TO A HIGH SHINE AND SET IT IN THEIR FRONT WINDOWS.

THEY PRUNE AND FEED IT TO KEEP IT IN BLOOM.

THEY JUST DON'T CALL IT EVIL.

KROOM

CASTING SHADOWS

A LOOK AT THE MAKING OF THE SHADOW: DEATH FACTORY FROM SCRIPT TO FINAL PAGE

script by PHIL HESTER
art by IVAN RODRIGUEZ
colors by IMPACTO STUDIOS
letters by ROB STEEN

PAGE TWO

PANEL ONE:
Money shot. The Shadow dives through the splintered door and down toward the camera, his guns forward and gleaming.

    SHADOW CAP: But I know.

    SHADOW: Hahahahaha!

PANEL TWO:
The Shadow lands in the center of the empty warehouse. Medium shot.

    SHADOW CAP: The Shadow knows.

    SHADOW: Haha--

PANEL THREE: The Shadow stands, his guns at his side. There's no one here. Make it clear that he expected to be interrupting a criminal enterprise that is not actually taking place. Th warehouse is completely bare. Almost a comical tableau.

    SHADOW (SMALL): Ha.

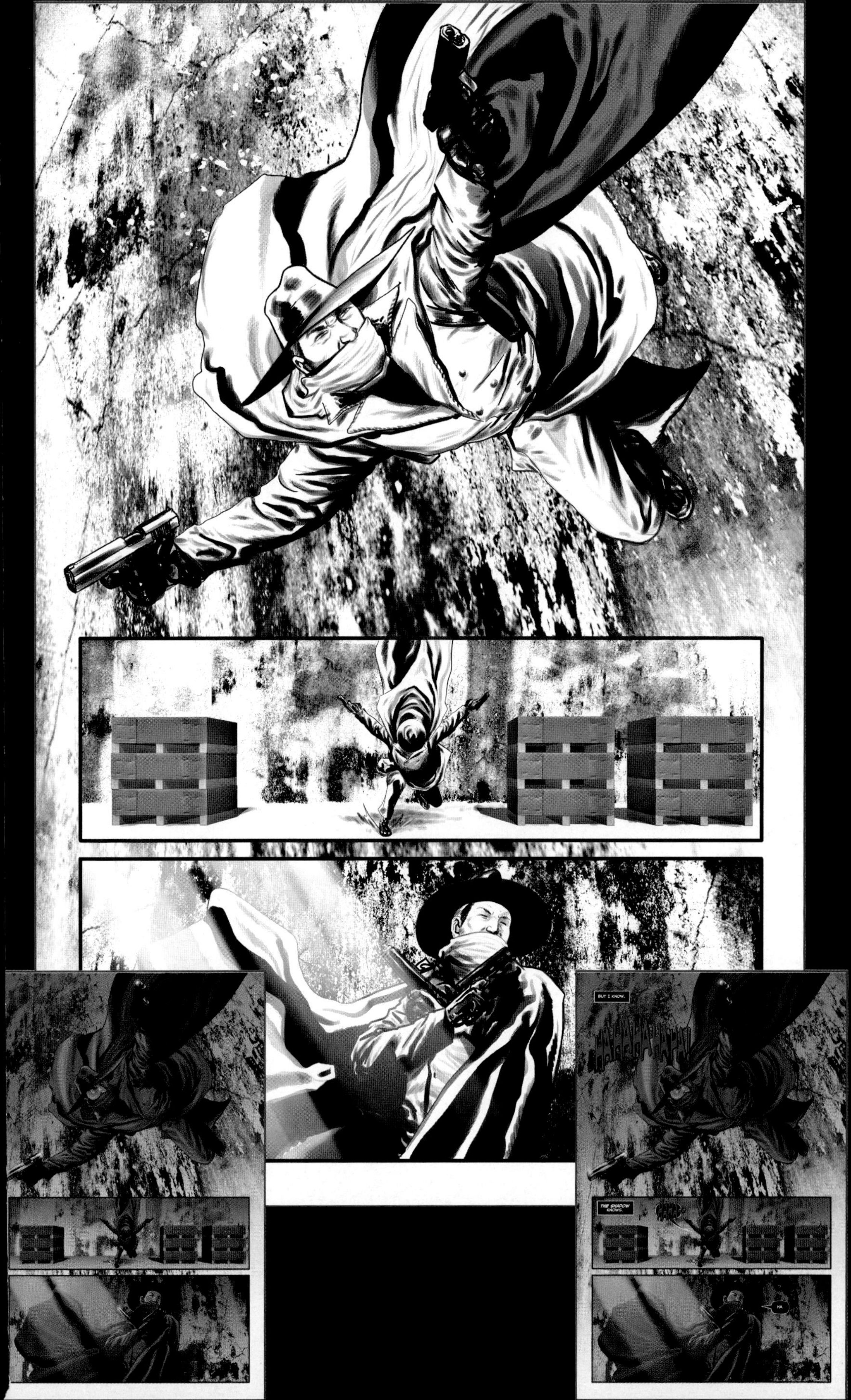
BUT I KNOW.
HAHAHAHAHA!
THE SHADOW KNOWS.
HA.

CASTING SHADOWS
A LOOK AT THE MAKING OF *THE SHADOW: DEATH FACTORY* FROM SCRIPT TO FINAL PAGE

script by PHIL HESTER
art by IVAN RODRIGUEZ
colors by IMPACTO STUDIOS
letters by ROB STEEN

PAGE THREE

PANEL ONE:
Cut to the streets of Manhattan in predawn gloaming. The streets are not busy. Focus on th
taxi cab of one of The Shadow's trusted agents, Shrevvy. See ref. We probably don't see it
yet, but The Shadow is Shrevvy's fare.

SHREVVY (FROM TAXI): "The Shadow knows?"

PANEL TWO:
Shot through the windshield to Shrevvy in driver's seat. He's got his eyebrows raised in a
confused expression. He's holding a Pulp magazine over the steering wheel, reading as he
drives. The magazine is called "The Shadow Detective Magazine" and features a comically
exaggerated version of The Shadow on the cover.

SHREVVY: You really say that sort of thing?

PANEL THREE:
Shrevvy looks back over his shoulder at The Shadow. There's an intersection in front of hir
but he doesn't seem concerned.

SHREVVY: You oughtta ride herd on this Maxwell Grant guy. I gotta tell you, some
times these stories get pretty weird.

PANEL FOUR   :
Profile shot of the cab as it weaves through the intersection, Shrevvy barely looking up fror
his magazine.

SHREVVY: I mean, in the last issue they said you could turn invisible and walk up
walls.

SHREVVY: And look at this one. It says you shot a guy so many times you sawed hi
body in half before it hit the ground.

PANEL FIVE:
Close on The Shadow glowering under his black brimmed hat.

SHADOW: True or not, the fables serve my purpose.

SHADOW: As long as they're sufficiently gruesome.

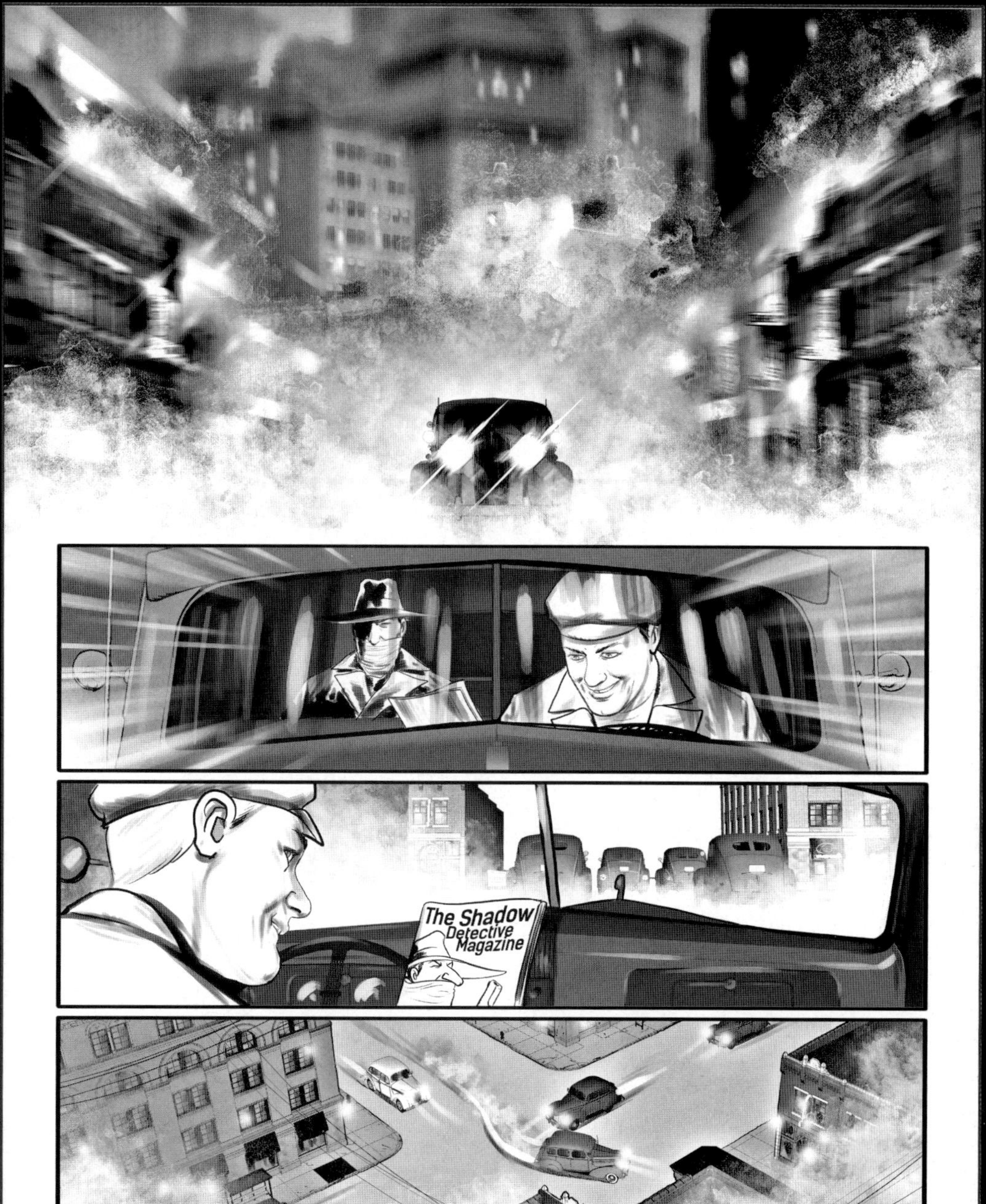
The Shadow
Detective
Magazine

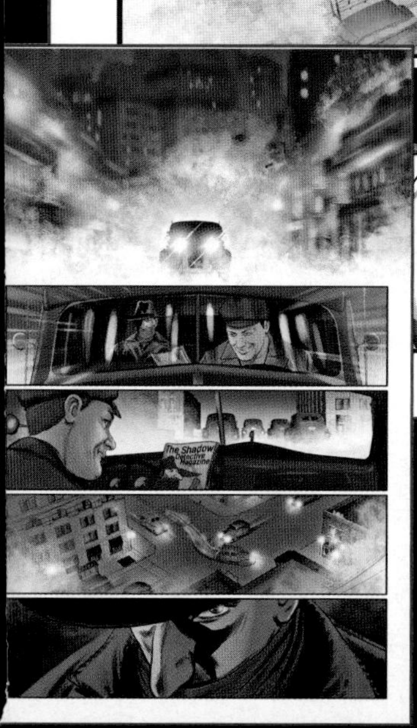
The Shadow
Detective
Magazine

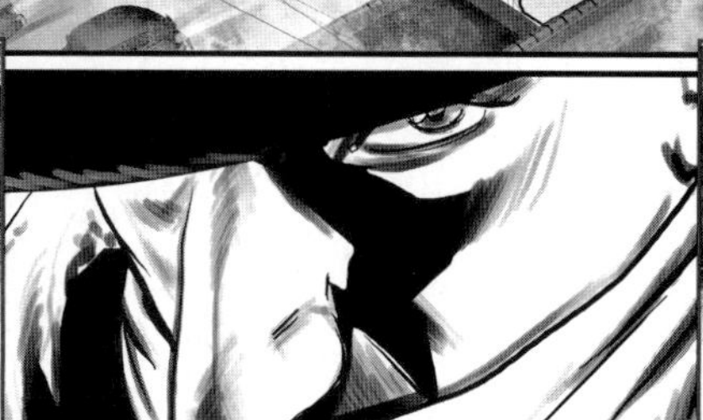

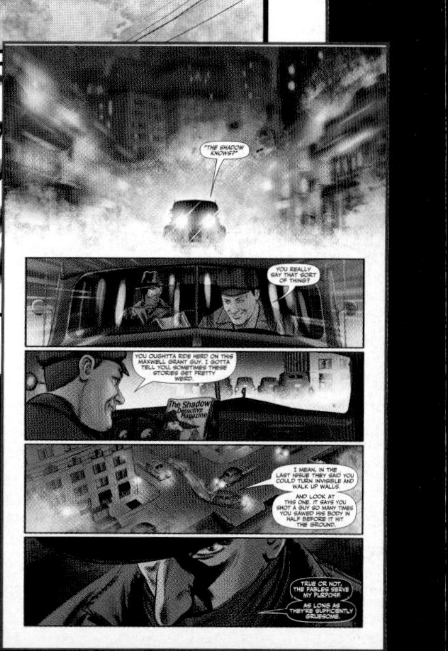
"THE SHADOW KNOWS?"
YOU REALLY SAY THAT SORT OF THING?
YOU OUGHTTA RIDE HERD ON THIS MAXWELL GRANT GUY. I GOTTA TELL YOU, SOMETIMES THESE STORIES GET PRETTY WEIRD.
The Shadow
Detective
Magazine
I MEAN, IN THE LAST ISSUE THEY SAID YOU COULD TURN INVISIBLE AND WALK UP WALLS.
AND LOOK AT THIS ONE. IT SAYS YOU SHOT A GUY SO MANY TIMES YOU SAWED HIS BODY IN HALF BEFORE IT HIT THE GROUND.
TRUE OR NOT, THE FABLES SERVE MY PURPOSE.
AS LONG AS THEY'RE SUFFICIENTLY GRUESOME.

CASTING SHADOWS

A LOOK AT THE MAKING OF THE COVER TO *THE SHADOW: DEATH FACTORY*

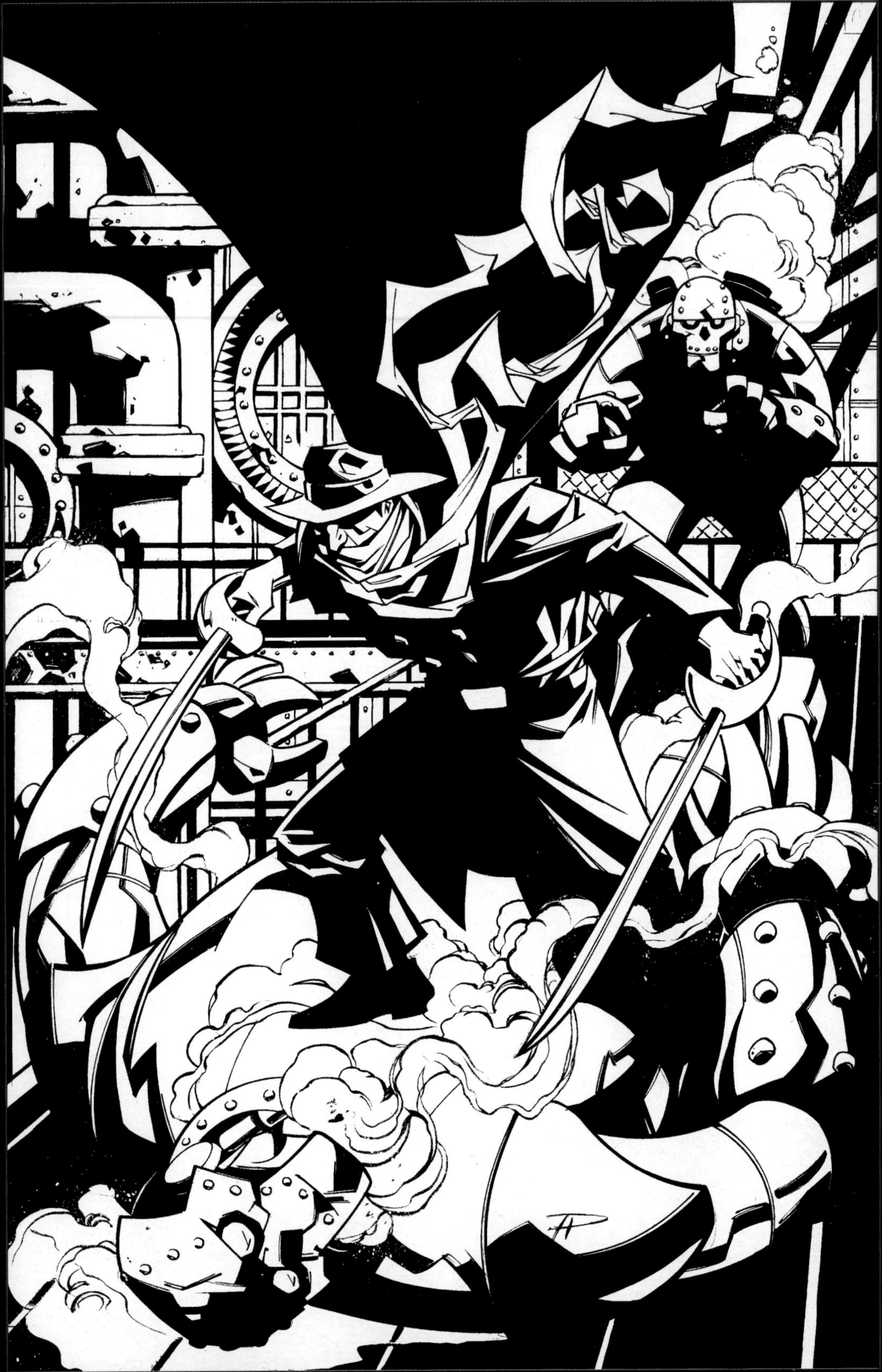

PHIL HESTER'S UNCOLORED INKS